CATHAR COUNTRY

By Michèle Aué
Translated by Simon Pleasance

LE PAYS CATHARE

MSM

THE title of this book deliberately alludes to concepts at once geographical and historical. "Cathar country" is no more nor less than the outcome of an association established between a land or *pays* and its history. What gives this book its unity is the Cathar phenomenon, here reviewed in all the tragic complexity resulting from a doctrine whose quest was purity, and which was finally snuffed out in the nightmare of a savage war of repression.

The geographical boundaries of Cathar country overlap with the region where this doctrine was played out. Its epicentre lies somewhere between Albi, the Lauragais, Minerve and the Corbières. But as it spread outward, it reached Languedoc, the Fenouillèdes district and even Catalonia to the south, the Plantaurel, Comminges and Agen Areas to the west, and the Quercy and Rouegue regions to the north, as well.

Cathar country is thus a vast lowland crescent ringed by the serried ranges of the Pyrénées to the south and the southernmost spurs of the Massif Central to the north. It is lent a certain unity by the magnificent thoroughfare of the lower Aude valley, which extends northwest along the middle reaches of the Garonne valley. This trail has been chosen by turns as the route for Roman roads, mail roads, the Canal du Midi, and modern highways and motorways. From Tautavel Man to the thriving metropolis of Toulouse, Cathar country has never dawdled. On the contrary, it has always kept abreast of history.

Fortresses perched high on dizzy-making pinnacles of rock have been given the specific name of "Cathar castles", even if their remains often predate the Cathar movement, and even if they have been put to use well after the last Cathar vanished. Montségur, Peyrepertuse, Quéribus, Puilaurens, Puivert, Roquefixade, Termes, and Carcassonne, these are the most resonant sites. But other places less directly haunted by those stakes where Cathars perished still guard deep within their heritage the vestiges, real or legendary, of a doctrine which helped to forge their identity.

In the Middle Ages, the language of Oc, once widely used, and enriched by the troubadours, gave rise to a brilliant culture founded on the celebration of courtly love. Today, as *Occitan,* it still endows a whole region with a powerful linguistic bond. But Cathar country is also that southerly part of France, the Midi, where placenames smack of fine wines and fine fare. Corbières, Rivesaltes, Fitou, Minervois, Limoux, Castelnaudary, Toulouse… a list handsome enough to be a sumptuous menu offered by Pantagruel.

If you take the time to gaze upon these landscapes, you will be a step nearer to understanding events that might seem strange or merely past history, were it not for the still visible traces of that past which preserve intact all their power of evocation and all their stirring mystery.

The keys to a secret

The Cathar theme thus provides the nub and structure of this book. To give the reader a better grasp of the interest and complexity of this religion, the first part offers a swift overview of the bases of the doctrine as well as a brief survey of the region's thrilling history throughout the 13th century. The second part of the book takes as its thread a spectacular journey round the most distinctive sites — and sights — in the region, from a geographical viewpoint as well as from a historical and cultural angle. But the journey is squarely underpinned by the magnetic force of the Cathar phenomenon.

This Cathar country tour takes in the foothills of the Pyrénées in a grand sweep from west to east. Then it ventures towards the Corbières and the Razès area, over Castelnaudary way, before heading east again towards Carcassonne, the Minervois, Narbonne and Béziers. From Foix to Montségur, by way of the famed Ariège caves, from the Aude gorge to Puilaurens, Peyrepertuse and Quéribus, not forgetting the magnificent abbeys of the Corbières and many other fine sites, it is a bountiful region indeed that this book would like you to discover.

1

THE CATHAR RELIGION

THE ALBIGENSIAN CRUSADE

The Cathar religion

The 10th and 11th centuries marked a period when religious sentiment intensified and became more demanding. The stance of the Catholic clergy no longer tallied with the idealized image of a simple and basic church that was evangelical and pure. Junior clergy were ill-trained and barely ventured into rural areas, while the wealth of the uppermost echelons, with their penchant for luxury, stood in stark contrast with the widespread poverty of their congregations.

The Church's responses failed to offer any proper solution to the doctrinal issues being raised by many Christians. As a result, groups of the faithful of their own accord set about finding satisfactory answers to their questions.

In 1163, Eckbert of Schönau, canon of Cologne cathedral, mockingly called these dissidents "Cathars", from the Greek *katharos*, meaning pure. The term "Albigensian" dates without any doubt from St. Bernard's mission to the Albi region in 1145. In 1165, in the small town of Lombers south of Albi, a well-attended debate organized by the Bishop of Albi pitted Catholics against Cathars. It was not until after this meeting that the name of "Albigensian" was properly applied to the Cathars, by then roundly accused of heresy and solemnly censured by the Catholic hierarchy.

The Cathar religion was a Christian religion

The Cathars believed in Christ, read the New Testament, with special emphasis on the Gospel according to St. John, and founded their belief on it. They even claimed to be the sole representatives of true Christianity. Their only prayer was the Paternoster.

The Cathar doctrine came about as a result of a distressing but inescapable assertion—that Good and Evil both have a share in the world. Whence a fundamental question: why

and how could or would an infinitely good and merciful God have created Evil, when God Himself is goodness infallible? In a nutshell: is Evil part and parcel of the divine creation? The Cathars came up with an answer to this soul-searching question.

The Cathar religion was founded on the age-old idea of dualism

This doctrine dates right back to Antiquity. It would seem to be closely linked with the ideas professed by members of 11th century Bulgarian sects called the Bogomils ("friends of God", from *bogo*: "God" and *mil*, "friend"). Further, in 1167 the Cathar Council of St. Félix-de-Caraman (now Saint-Félix-Lauragais) was chaired by the Bogomil deacon Nicetas. On the contrary, symbolic themes of Bogomil inspiration have been erroneously attributed to the Cathars.

Dualism is based on a simple notion. Two principles are at odds: Good and Evil. There is but one God, the God of Good, creator of the everlasting kingdom of the spirit, whence come souls, the sparks of life.

Evil is merely a lower principle that has created the "World", in other words, matter and time. It strives to do away with the kingdom of Good. To this end, it encloses a small part of life (the soul) in a material package (the body), and invents time (duration), the essential principle of corruption and destruction.

Man thus stands at the crossroads of these two principles. His soul belongs to the kingdom of Good, his body to the corrupted world here below. For the Cathars, salvation involved freeing oneself from the world of Evil, which was likened to hell, and reaching the kingdom of Good, fully cognizant.

The Cathar religion was a religion of knowledge, and revelation

The Cathars did not expect death to offer their souls automatic deliverance. The soul can only enter the kingdom of Good if it has regained its original purity, in other words, cognizance of its divine origin.

It is Christ, sent to Earth by God, who revealed this key to salvation to man. This knowledge could only be received during baptism by the laying on of hands and by the Holy Spirit: the *consolamentum*. This spiritual baptism gave the Cathars an "understanding of Good". It retained the three roles of revelation, ordination and extreme unction within the history of Catharism. The laying on of hands by which this baptism was passed to the new member symbolized the entry into religious life and the recognition of the Holy Spirit by the soul imprisoned within a body made of flesh. The *consolamentum* could only be conferred by a person who had already been "consoled"—a "good Christian", a *perfectus* or a *perfecta*.

The Cathars were not afraid of death because, for them, hell was on Earth. So it should come as no surprise that, in 1244, men and women at Montségur elected, with admirable bravery, to face death at the stake already prepared for them at the foot of the rock.

The Cathar religion was a tireless quest for Christian perfection

The rules of conduct governing Cathar life were borrowed straight from the Gospels and applied strictly to the letter:

— "Thou shalt not kill": each and every body, be it human or animal, is a fleshly frame which may be occupied by a soul awaiting salvation. Cathars also refused to eat meat and any other animal-based food (eggs, butter, milk etc.).

— Fasting was obligatory: the "good Christian" must be detached from the material world, the world of Evil. The spiritual nourishment of the soul completely surpasses the material food of the body, the work of Evil.

— Abstention from sexual intercourse: procreation is the work of Evil, because it creates a fleshly frame which imprisons a soul.

Perfecti and believers

Those Cathars at the most advanced stage of detachment from the material world received the consolamentum. They were traditionally called perfecti, although they themselves did not use this term. They preferred to be called, more simply, "good people" (bons hommes), "good Christians", or, like the Bogomils of Bulgaria, "friends of God". They were bound to lead a life of exemplary asceticism. Work, prayer and preaching were the main tasks of the perfecti, who were encompassed by the Holy Ghost.

Attired in dark linen cloth, they travelled about in pairs, exercising the rules of the Cathar ethic to the absolute letter. The perfectae, who were educated and often cultured women, also played an important part in the Cathar system. They ran "houses" akin to convents where Cathar girls were brought up, and unaccompanied women would find shelter. Work was their major activity, whatever their social status.

But not all Cathars were perfecti. The great majority of them were "believers"— laypersons who had espoused the faith and were striving to attain the state of purity achieved by the perfecti.

They were still under the sway of the principle of Evil, and thus prone to sin. When they died, they would receive the "consolamentum of the dying". This differed from the rite accorded to the perfecti, for it offered "believers" no more than the chance of a "good end", in other words, reincarnation of the soul in a new fleshly frame, and thus another chance of salvation.

When the Albigensian Crusade entered its most cruel and tragic stages, some believers drew up a kind of pact with the elders of the Cathar Church. This pact called the convenensa guaranteed that they would be "consoled" at the moment of their death, even if they had already lost consciousness.

At the end of the 13th century, the "consolamentum of the dying" might also be supplemented by the endura. This was a total fast leading inexorably to death. It thus enabled the faithful to know for sure that they would have the "good end" assured them by the "consolamentum of the dying". Should they recover, it also prevented them from rejoining the world of sin and Evil.

A page from the Cathar rite, in Occitan ▶

eā ex uolūtate uiri · s; ex deo
ati s̄ · Et ūbū caro factū est ·
t abitauit ī nobis · Uidimus
ā eius · glā q̄si unigeniti a
re · Plenū gracie ⁊ ūitatis ·
hs testimoniū ꝑhibet de ipō · e
clamabat dicens · hic est q̄m
xi · q̄ post me uēturus est · ā
me fact⁹ est · q̄ prior me erat
at · Et d plenitudine eius n
omīs acce pim⁹ grām ꝓ grā · q̄a
per moysen data est · grā e
tas p ihm xp̄m facta est ·

Os eni
uēgut
dnaut
du · ed
nāt u
os · ede
nāt la
ded na
mīt de
gisia precep⁹ fuissi · e pdo · e
ecclesia · d tuit li nr̄s pecat li
uem fait indis · in p esgat · m
atz dl nr̄e naissemēt ēt fi na

eza · cē ī rem nr̄a adu · Lauos que
nos ꝑguetz p nos lo paire · s̄ ·
d nr̄a ēnos p do ·

Adorem deu e manifeste tuit
lumie pecat · e las nr̄as mo
utas greus ofensios · d per gar
danit dl paire edlsti · edl onora
s̄ · esprit · edls onoratz sanhs an
āgels · edls onoratz s̄ · apostols ·
P la orō · e pla se · e pla saluatō · d
tuit ll diters glosses creitas · e
dls bonauratz ourmitz āce sore e
dels fizels enauiro estāt · ed nāt
nos · s̄ · senho ēnos pdonetz tot go
ēa nos pecām · būdicite parcite ōbs ·

Quar moutz soles nr̄es pe
catz els q̄ls nos ofēde āni
cadia · pnuit e perdia · ē paraū
la · ē obra e ses ō cossirer · a bno
lōtat e senes uolōtat · e p ꝑ
la nr̄a uolotat · la q̄l d nāt nos
a pera tā les malignis espitz en
las cārs que uestem · būdici
te parcite nobis ·

Mdu ai cula sca paraula
d d u nos ēbha eu · s̄ · a

— A ban on taking oaths and preaching sermons: this precept was taken from the Gospel according to St. Matthew. Thirteenth century society, of course, was based on procreation and obedience to the oath of loyalty. Sworn ties of vassalage were the crucial cogs of the social structure.

— Work was a given: this obligation applied to all the Cathar faithful, even those of noble birth.

In addition to these rules, believers were expected to:

— attend sermons given by *perfecti*.

— show marks of respect to any *perfecti* encountered by practising the *melioramentum*— bowing three times to the ground and asking the *perfecti* for their blessing.

All ceremonies invariably ended with the "kiss of peace" or "charity". This was exchanged between *perfecti* and believers, and sym-

Cathars and weavers

Cathars often plied the trade of merchant or weaver. In the Middle Ages, Languedoc was an important cloth-manufacturing region. In the 13th century, cloth mills spread, serving also as propaganda outlets for the new faith.

It is a fact, for example, that Cordes owed its prosperity to the influx of Cathar weavers who sought refuge in the town. These new resident Cathars organized active resistance groups, if we are to believe the tale of the three inquisi-

tors who visited Cordes to execute their much-feared mission, but ended up dead at the bottom of a well.

Similarly, the Mas-Cabardès "Weavers' Cross" is thought by some to be of Cathar origin. There is little real proof for any such identification, but it still conjures up the link existing between the weaver's trade and the heretical sect—so much so that Occitan *tesseyre*, meaning weaver, soon became synonymous with Cathar.

Cordes

The Pater noster stairway at Cordes

The Mas-Cabardès «Weavers' Cross»

bolized the spiritual communion of the gathering.

Was Catharism a purified form of Christianity or a heresy?

The sole recognized sacrament was the *consolamentum* or initiatory baptism. This had to do with neither purification nor revelation. It involved contemplation, faith, and assent, and could only be administered to adults. Children were in no case eligible, and the newborn even less so.

Jesus is not Christ the Redeemer, but rather a revealer and saviour. He was the first to perform the baptism by the Holy Spirit, as it was proclaimed by John the Baptist.

The Cathars rejected the Eucharist: bread and wine could not represent Christ's flesh and blood—the carnal frame. Christ's words were to be understood as the broadcasting of a spiritual knowledge, not of a communion with the divine principle.

Fanjeaux: discoid cross

As an instrument of Jesus' agony, the Cross could not be worshipped. The Greek cross inscribed within a circle, and the many-branched solar cross, have often been attributed to the cathars as symbolic themes. In reality, however, the Cathars apparently never made the visible sacred in any physical symbol.

The miracles worked by Christ should be understood at a spiritual level, and interpreted as allegories. The material world is the work of Evil, and cannot be rectified.

Essentially, then, Catharism was a Christian religion, even though the Catholic powers-that-be managed to see it as a heresy, and thus a dangerous deviation. What is more, the Cathar doctrine undermined the very foundations of the feudal society in which the Catholic Church played such an integral part.

To start with, the Catholic Church tried to check the advances of the heresy from the pulpit. When these far-reaching efforts proved to be to no avail, the Church organized a bitter military campaign akin to a holy war.

St. Bernard

St. Bernard, a friar at Cîteaux, was the founder of Clairvaux Abbey, cradle of the Cistercian Reformation. In 1145 he took part in a preaching mission in Toulouse, Albi and Verfeil. The aim: to fight the spread of heretical teachings in these parts.

His mission enjoyed a favourable reception in Toulouse and in Albi, but things in Verfeil went less smoothly. He took to task the local barons, accused of backing the heresy, who had left the church in droves, followed by much of the local congregation. The preacher carried his sermons into the public square, but the townspeople locked themselves in their homes and created such an uproar that he was soon forced to give up. St. Bernard proceeded to trample the ground underfoot, kicking up the dust to show the people that they, too, would soon return to dust once more. On the point of leaving Verfeil, his mission having failed, St. Bernard loudly cursed the village: "May God wither thee, Verfeil!"—a thinly veiled pun, for in Latin Verfeil means "green leaf".

The history
of the Albigensian Crusade

Languedoc in the 13th century

The regions where Occitan, the language of *oc*, was spoken were under the sway of various princes. As the royal power waned throughout the Carolingian period, so the power and independence of these princes had waxed. The Capetian kings were unable to improve the situation. So in the early 13th century the political position in Occitania was a complex one.

The counts of Toulouse, in conjunction with Raymond VI of Saint-Gilles, ruled over a four-sided domain, encompassing the Garonne Valley, the Rouergue and Quercy regions, and possessions in upper Provence.

The counts of Barcelona, in the person of Peter II of Aragon, controlled the Pyrenees, Catalonia, Aragon, and Provence, and had recently received homages from the counts of Bigorre and Béarn.

Wedged between these two power blocs were the Trencavels, viscounts of Béziers. They had built their own princedom from Carcassonne to Béziers, skilfully juggling with the rivalry between the lords of Toulouse and Aragon. They were vassals of Toulouse, but since 1179 had paid solemn homage to Aragon!

Further north, Philip II Augustus, king of France, was busily trying to establish a strong royal domain, founded on ever larger territorial gains. In Rome, meanwhile, pope Innocent III, an active, energetic pontiff, was showing increasing alarm at the advances being made by the Cathar heresy in Languedoc.

The four major Cathar "dioceses"—Agen, Albi, Carcassonne and Toulouse—overlapped almost exactly with the holdings of the powerful feudal barons of the South. Some local lords had lent their backing to the heretics, enabling them to outwit the incompetent clergy,

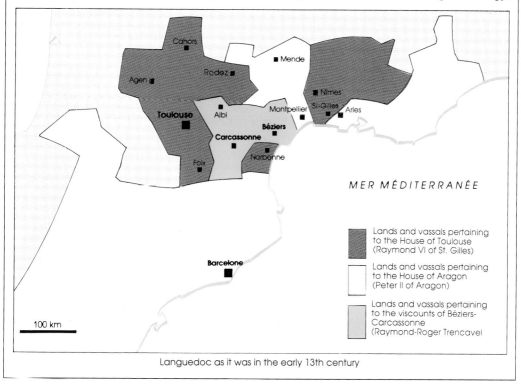

Lands and vassals pertaining to the House of Toulouse (Raymond VI of St. Gilles)

Lands and vassals pertaining to the House of Aragon (Peter II of Aragon)

Lands and vassals pertaining to the viscounts of Béziers-Carcassonne (Raymond-Roger Trencavel)

Languedoc as it was in the early 13th century

◀ Toulouse: the "palm tree" o fan-vaulting in the Church of the Jacobins

particularly as a result of the exemplary model posed by the *perfecti*. There were not many *perfecti*, a thousand odd perhaps. Be that as it may, even if only 10-15% of the populace were really influenced by the heresy, as seems likely, it was nevertheless tolerated, and often supported, by much of the population.

It was this that alarmed the Catholic hierarchy, and pope Innocent III in particular. For he sensed the virus that might destroy the unity of Christianity in the West.

From pulpit to crusade

In 1206, canon Dominico Guzman (later to become St. Dominic) started to preach against the Cathar heresy throughout the South. He was zealous and forthright, but was forced to admit that his efforts were to little avail. In something akin to a prophetic vision, he foretold the grievous events about to overtake Languedoc: "I have preached, I have entreated, I have wept...the rod must now do the work of benediction. Towers will be torn down, walls toppled, and ye shall be reduced to bondage. This is how might shall prevail where meekness has failed." Not long thereafter, things took an abrupt turn for the worse.

At the very dawn of the 13th century, Innocent III had appointed a contingent of legates, whose mission was to reform the local clergy and combat the Cathar heresy. The first two papal legates were two monks from Fontfroide Abbey: Peter of Castelnau and Friar Raoul.

Peter of Castelnau was assassinated in 1208 not far from Saint-Gilles, in somewhat mysterious circumstances. His murder provided the Catholic authorities with a perfect pretext for organizing an armed campaign against the heretical Cathars. Innocent III reacted straightaway. He openly accused Raymond of Saint-Gilles, count of Toulouse, of being at the root of the killing, and excommunicated him. At the same time, throughout Christendom, he incited his flock to mount a crusade against the Cathar heretics.

The noblemen and knights who "took up the cross" became players in a holy war against the heretics—a war that was likened to a battle to be waged against the infidel in some holy land. Those taking part enjoyed the same privileges: remission of sins and the promise of paradise for any soldier dying in battle. A specific supplementary clause was added: the estates of the powerful southern vassals guilty of collaboration with the heretics would be "regarded as booty"—in a word, they would legally belong to the first crusader to take them for himself. This measure seemed to be tantamount to unabashed meddling by the Catholic Church in the purely political and feudal affairs of the French kingdom. The pope was redistributing land already handed out by the kings of France to some of their vassals. Philip II Augustus was under no illusions and refused to take any personal part in the crusade, though he authorized his vassals to take up the cause.

Who exactly were the crusaders? On the whole, they were barons from the north of the kingdom (Ile-de-France, Champagne, Flanders, Burgundy) come to take up arms in the handsome provinces of the South. Some of them nurtured secret hopes of carving out new fiefdoms for themselves in these rich southerly lands. Others were acting simply in obeisance to their suzerain, the king of France. But they were nonetheless resolved not to spend more than the standard forty days of their military service in Languedoc. Their number included such notables as Eudes, duke of Burgundy, Hervé, count of Nevers, Gaucher of Chatillon, and many more. In their wake came a host of "footmen", orderlies, carpenters, crossbowmen and archers, who formed the traditional entourage in the service of powerful noblemen. Then there were the roving bands that tagged on to every mediaeval cavalcade—rogues, ruffians, knaves and vagrants who joined in every underhand move, all eager to plunder and kill.

Arnaud Amaury, abbot of Cîteaux and papal legate, was religious head of the expedition.

The Albigensian Crusade

The crusading knights and their retinues headed southwards along the classic thoroughfare—the Rhone valley.

Raymond VI of Toulouse, now excommunicated, sensed the danger posed to his estates. He publicly repented and, to prove his good faith, took up the cross in his turn. Trencavel, count of Béziers and viscount of Carcassonne was keen to do likewise. But the crusaders turned him down, reckoning that their crusade would lose all rhyme and reason if all the southern nobility took up the cross. What is more, they decided to attack Béziers...

The sack of Béziers

On 21 July 1209, the crusading army stood looking across the river Orb at the city beyond, clustered proudly about its cathedral. The young Trencavel was away organizing the defence of Carcassonne. The people of Béziers bravely refused the crusaders' invitation to hand over any Cathars within "to avoid sharing their fate and perishing with them."

A lengthy siege seemed in the offing. But the crusaders managed to enter the city by means of a surprise attack. They mercilessly and indiscriminately massacred the inhabitants, Cathars and Catholics alike. And did Arnaud Amaury really utter those famous words as the crusaders launched their assault: "Slay them all. God will recognize his people..."? It matters little now. Like all of history's neat sayings, it summarizes within a memorable sentence a whole state of mind.

The crusade got off to a bad start for the people of the South. The crusaders reckoned that a slaughter of such magnitude should serve as an example. It would obviate any future need for long and costly sieges, as well as bloody, destructive onslaughts. It should be remembered that the crusaders had come to seize the lands and cities of the South. They were thus keen for them to be in good order, and still brimming with their riches.

The fall of Carcassonne

Early in the month of August 1209, flushed from their victory at Béziers, the crusaders marched on Carcassonne. Trencavel had prepared his city's defences. He had a handsome stronghold on top of a naturally fortified hill, encircled by stout walls punctuated by thirty towers and more. The crusaders attacked from the north and took control of the water sources supplying the city. The siege closed in around the ramparts. Carcassonne started to suffer from heat, thirst and fear—the classic ingredients of a slow and agonizing death. Then Trencavel decided to negotiate. His surrender still remains an enigma. At the negotiating table he was taken prisoner and tossed into the deepest dungeon in the citadel. On 10 November, Raymond Roger Trencavel died in prison, poisoned—according to some—by his enemies. He was 24. Carcassonne was taken. The inhabitants were routed, fleeing almost naked, with no money or chattels, taking with them—in the words of Pierre des Vaux de Cernay—just their sins. Fiction—or might it be fact?—has it that the citizenry fled through an underground passage that surfaced 12 miles north of the city, at the foot of the castles of Lastours, owned by Pierre Roger de Cabaret, a Trencavel vassal. But there is no sure way of checking this far-fetched hypothesis, and, whatever the case, the walled city of Carcassonne emerged from this fearsome siege considerably the weaker.

Raymond VI, count of Toulouse, witnessed these bloody goings-on from the crusaders' camp, as a mere onlooker. He did not in fact play any direct part in the destruction of the viscounty of the Trencavels. Their estates, "regarded as booty", would be handed over to a crusading knight of the Catholic faith. The leading barons were well aware of the precedent that was being set, and refused to strip one of

their number of his possessions—even if he was a southerner suspected of heresy! Moreover, they were all vassals of the king of France, and were therefore reluctant to set themselves against him in the event of any dispute over possession of the Languedoc estates.

In the end, it was a lordling from Ile-de-France who accepted both the lands and titles of the viscount of Carcassonne. His name was Simon de Montfort.

The exploits of Simon de Montfort

The conquests of the crusading knights proceeded, now headed by Simon de Montfort, his ambitions forever gaining pace.

He marched on Montréal and Fanjeaux—where he met St. Dominic, Limoux and Castres where the first Cathar stake was lit, Cabaret—which resisted and did not fall, Mirepoix, where he installed his loyal friend Guy de Lévis, Pamiers, Saverdun, Lombers and Albi, which all fell into his hands.

Old dwellings in Castres

The collegiate church at Montréal

In the spring of 1210, the crusaders made their way unopposed into Alzonne, abandoned by its inhabitants. The people of Bram bravely resolved to fight the crusaders and set about defending their walled village. But the siege only lasted three days before Bram surrendered.

Simon de Montfort then decided to mete out an exemplary punishment to the rebels standing in his way. From his prisoners, he selected a hundred men, gouged out their eyes, and cut off their ears, lips and noses. One particular prisoner was "merely" blinded in one eye so that he could lead his companions to the most renowned castle in the region, the fortress of Cabaret, still defying the crusading armies from the height of its crag.

When the bedraggled troop arrived there, it was meant to spread alarm and terror. Instead, it merely fired the determination and courage of the southerners. Cabaret held out.

The fall of the Cathar strongholds

Simon de Montfort laid siege to Minerve in June 1210. Surrounded by deep gorges and ravines, the fortified village was defended by a skilled and able garrison led by William of Minerve. After a six-week siege, the village fell, but not because of the battery of engines of war wielded by the crusaders. Its demise, as at Carcassonne, was due to thirst, for cannonballs had destroyed access to the water sources. The village surrendered, but the garrison was spared. Not so the 140 Cathars who refused to renounce their faith and were burnt alive. Legend has it that they hurled themselves of their own accord on to the blazing stake.

Simon de Montfort took heart from his victory over Minerve, and decided to attack the imposing fortress at Termes. It took a four-month siege to take it. The apparently impregnable fortress, perched on its pinnacle of solid rock, was defended by Raymond of Termes. Once more, the defeat of the citadel was due to a shortage of drinking water. When dysentery started to wreak havoc among the defending ranks, Termes finally fell to Simon de Montfort.

It took no more than a three-day siege before Simon de Montfort took Puivert castle. After the fall of Termes and Puivert, Pierre Roger de Cabaret, lord of Lastours, decided to hand over his castles to the commander of the crusade. In the spring of 1211, Simon de Montfort took possession of the four castles, spared the bitter fight that he feared he would have to put up. Now he could launch a direct attack on the two most powerful lords in the region, the counts of Toulouse and Foix. Before doing so, however, he had to take hold of various vital strongholds, such as the fortress of Lavaur, where a large band of Cathars had taken refuge.

Raymond VI

The count of Toulouse, Raymond VI, was a contradictory figure whose stance during the course of the Albigensian Crusade often appeared ambivalent. As a Catholic, his donations to the abbeys in his countship seemed offered in all sincerity, but he also showed an alarming tolerance towards the large numbers of heretics on his estates. Raymond VI was eventually excommunicated, charged with heresy and complicity in the murder of Peter of Castelnau.

Early in the year 1211, he must have felt very deeply torn between his desire to remain obedient to the Church as a good Christian, and his reluctance to take up arms against his own Cathar subjects, for whom he clearly felt an unmistakable sympathy.

From 1209 onward, when he took up the cross, the situation in Languedoc had changed a great deal. The crusaders were occupying much of the country, and exercising direct sway over the lands of Occitania. Raymond VI found the idea of fighting against the Cathars unacceptable, even if the penalty for not doing so involved losing his authority and sovereignty over his own possessions, which then came under the strict laws of the crusading barons. From that point on, the schism between the Catholic crusaders and the count of Toulouse was inevitable.

The raiding crusaders

The crusading armies scoured the South, going wherever there was a battle to wage.

Most major towns in the Quercy region and along the Garonne valley—Agen, Moissac, Montauban, Castelsarrasin, Caussade, Caylus, Saint-Antonin-Noble-Val, Villemur, Cahors, Puylaurens, and Penne d'Agenais—were visited by Simon de Montfort's armies. Indeed, his fighting men rode as far as Rocamadour and even to the gates of Rodez...

The environs of Albi were also the arena for many a battle—at Albi, Gaillac, Rabastens, Cadalen, Penne d'Albigeois, Roquemaure, Ceystarols, and even around Castres and Graulhet.

In the Toulousain, Lauragais, Carcassès and Razès areas, as well as the Corbières, battles became too numerous to list. Every town can trace some episode from the *Hystoria Albigensis* in its past.

Last but not least, the Pyrenees were not trodden underfoot as systematically as the lowlands by the crusaders, but forays were all the same mounted in the foothills against towns like Tarascon-sur-Ariège, Lavelanet, Foix, and even Lourdes.

Penne d'Albigeois

The cloister at Moissac

◄ Rocamadour

The siege of Lavaur

In the spring of 1211, the crusaders reached the ramparts of Lavaur and mounted a taxing siege. By 3 May, however, after much fierce fighting, they entered the town.

Terrible repression ensued. Eighty knights had their throats slit. Bowed by the weight of one such knight, Aymeri of Montréal—a colossus of a man, the gallows snapped! Dame Guiraude took an active part in the defence of her town, but finally fell into the hands of the crusaders: "Screaming, sobbing and yelling, she was hurled into a well. There, she was buried beneath stones, much to the dismay of the crowd [...] It was a great sorrow and crime, for Dame Guiraude was a good and charitable lady". So reads the Song of the Crusade. Three or four hundred Cathars were captured and thrown into the flames of the largest stake of the entire crusade. The chroniclers' exact figures differ, but they are all agreed that " they were most numerous." Some days later, the crusaders again showed the measure of their cruelty at Les Cassés, where some sixty Cathars were burnt at the stake. Next, without delay, Simon de Montfort laid siege to Toulouse, but foundered. Since the siege of Lavaur, Raymond VI and Roger Bernard, count of Foix, had decided to join forces against the crusaders. The commitment now was no longer religious, but political. It was war between North and South, no more, no less.

North and South clash at Castelnaudary

For the first time, the southern barons amalgamated to confront the crusaders. The crunch came at Castelnaudary in September 1211. Here, after many a bloody and murderous battle, both sides claimed victory. But a serious threat still menaced the southerners. Theirs was a fragile coalition, and it wavered after this inconclusive battle.

The cross of the stake at Lavaur

The cross of Les Cassés

The battle of Muret

In September 1213, Simon de Montfort decided to attack Muret castle. It was a long siege, for reinforcements could not now be called up on the same huge scale as at the start of the crusade. Peter II, king of Aragon and count of Barcelona, was alarmed at the ever burgeoning ambitions of the crusaders' commander-in-chief, and resolved to go to war. He allied his troops with those of Raymond VI, and attacked the crusading armies which were laying siege to Muret. The battle of 12 September 1213 beneath the town walls was savage. Amid the turmoil of hand-to-hand combat, Peter II of Aragon was slain. In the tradition of true chivalry, his death spread dismay through the ranks of the Aragonese nobility. Raymond VI and his men withdrew to Toulouse. Simon de Montfort was once more triumphant.

The aftermath of the disastrous defeat at Muret was extremely serious. The South buckled. Foix, Narbonne and Comminges all fell into the hands of Simon de Montfort. The crusaders marched into Toulouse in 1215. Count Raymond VI and his son, were beaten and opted to flee into exile at the English court, well removed from the French realm.

The death of Simon de Montfort

In July 1216, when news spread that Innocent III—the pope who had launched the crusade—was dead, Raymond VII-to-be decided to regain the lands that had belonged to the countship. He paraded in Toulouse, and the city rose up and routed the crusading knights. On 13 September 1217, his father, Raymond VI, in turn entered his proud city of Toulouse. This enraged Simon de Montfort. He rallied his troops before the city, which proceeded to suffer its second siege. It promised to be a lengthy one, but in June 1218, after several months of fighting, a stone projected by a mangonel struck Simon de Montfort in the head. The "Lion of the Crusade" collapsed, mortally wounded.

The crusade runs out of steam

Simon de Montfort's son, Amaury, tried to carry on and further his father's good works, but failed in the task. He had no option but to call off the siege of Toulouse. When their forty days of service in the crusade were over, the northern barons gradually rejoined their domains in Ile-de-France. The count of Toulouse and his Occitan vassals slowly regained pos-

Simon de Montfort

Simon IV de Montfort, also known as Simon the Strong, was born in 1150 or thereabouts. He was lord of Montfort and Epernon.

In 1209, when he decided to join the crusade mounted by the pope against the Cathar heresy, he was close on sixty years old.

Pierre des Vaux de Cernay sketched a portrait of him that would do credit to any valiant knight of yore. Fired by a mission in which he passionately believed, for almost nine years he headed a ruthless campaign in the provinces of southern France. His religious fervour was matched only by his bravery, yet he bequeathed the image of an ambitious conqueror and a cruel warrior.

So it was quite natural that the people of Toulouse should proclaim most loudly their joy and their relief when his death was announced in 1218. He was killed by a stone-throwing engine of war, well-positioned on the walls of Toulouse, and operated, so the story goes, by women and girls. This is how Pierre des Vaux de Cernay described it: "And the stone came right for him, in the right spot, and struck the count so accurately on his steel helmet that his eyes, brain, teeth, forehead and jaw broke into smithereens. He fell to the ground, dead, bleeding and black."

Chroniclers of the crusade have used a multitude of adjectives to capture the nature of an undoubtedly exceptional man—gallant, kindly, valiant, fair, or, conversely, cruel, murderous and bloodthirsty. Whichever adjectives are right, he certainly earned his nickname of "Lion of the Crusade".

session of the lands confiscated from them. Amaury de Montfort was unable to contain this liberation movement, and donated all the lands taken by his father to the king of France.

He marched out of Carcassonne for the last time, in defeat, on 15 January 1224, taking with him his father's corpse sewn into an ox-hide so that his tomb, in the church of St. Nazaire in Carcassonne, would not be desecrated by the foe. As the crusade ran out of steam, so the Cathar heresy found new vigour.

It was at this juncture, and in quick succession, that death claimed three of the leading protagonists in this savage conflict. In 1222, Raymond VI, count of Toulouse, passed away. Then the year 1223 saw the passing of both Roger Bernard, count of Foix, and Philip II Augustus, king of France.

Louis VIII's royal crusade

Philip II Augustus had never been keen to take an active part in the Albigensian Crusade. His son, Louis VIII, urged on by his ambitious wife, Blanche of Castile, joined the crusade against Raymond VII, who had been officially declared an "enemy of King and Church."

Louis VIII's arrival in Languedoc in 1226 triggered a wave of surrenders among the major towns and cities of the South. The viscounty of Carcassonne was annexed to the kingdom of France, but the countships of Toulouse and Foix, as well as the viscounties of Narbonne and the Fenouillèdes district further south remained independent. For Blanche of Castile, it was clear that these lands would one day belong to the French crown. After Louis VIII's death, in 1226, she invested all her energies and skills to achieve this end.

The capitulation of Raymond VII and the Treaty of Meaux

In 1229, Raymond VII met the regent Blanche of Castile in Meaux, this latter acting in the name of her young son, king Louis IX (later to become St. Louis). The speed with which Raymond VII capitulated before the king and the Church was astonishing.

The young prince had displayed such courage and ability in his fight against the crusading knights, and here he now was bowing to all the demands and humiliation meted out to him by the regent and the papal legate, Romain de Saint-Ange, in exchange for his absolution, which was publicly received in Paris. The count of Toulouse was thus obliged to take part in the struggle against the Cathar heresy.

The court of the Inquisition

In 1233, pope Gregory IX established a religious institution destined to enjoy a thriving future: the infamous Inquisition. Its purpose was better to apply the clauses of the Treaty of Meaux. These courts were headed by panels of Dominican monks, their order having latterly been created by St. Dominic. Their specific task was to try heretics. The statutory penalty was the stake. In effect, this arrangement merely rendered official a practice that was already widespread, though somewhat illegal.

Cathar resistance

Little by little a resistance movement sprang up based near mighty strongholds such as Montségur and Quéribus. The Cathars, who had gathered for a synod at Montségur in 1232, asked Raymond of Pereille to prepare defences around his castle, so that it might serve as a refuge for persecuted groups of Cathars. The three major castles of the Fenouillèdes district—Puilaurens, Peyrepertuse and Quéribus—were all reputed to be impregnable. The heretics took refuge in them, to escape the clutches of the inquisitors.

Some *perfecti*, however, did not hesitate to emerge from their fortresses to "console" those dying in the lowland areas around Carcassonne and Toulouse. For a long time, Guilhabert of Castres thwarted the traps laid by the inquisitors, moving freely around the Lauragais and Toulouse regions, preaching to "believers" carrying on their worship in utmost clandestinity.

During the summer of 1240, the young viscount Raymond, son of Raymond Roger Trencavel, who had died in 1209, reformed an army with the help of various faydit[1] barons and attempted to retake his old domains. He gained possession of several castles but, despite a testing siege at Carcassonne, he failed to take the walled city, fleeing first to Montréal and then Aragon.

On 16 November 1240, after lengthy negotiations, Lord William of Peyrepertuse surrendered his citadel to the king of France. The awe-inspiring stronghold high on its pinnacle of rock was no longer a match for the crusading army.

1- Languedoc noblemen dispossessed or exiled because of their allegiance during the Crusade.

The Avignonet affair

The courts of the Inquisition were so merciless, and their extortions so extreme, that, in May 1242, two grand inquisitors and their attendants were assassinated in Avignonet by men who had slipped out of Montségur castle.

Blanche of Castile and Louis IX made the most of the incident to order a fight to the bitter end against the rebels of Languedoc. It would seem that Raymond VII, count of Toulouse was more guilty than not in the Avignonet affair.

In January 1243, he was forced to beg for forgiveness and swear loyalty to the king of France. As far as the Inquisition was concerned, Avignonet remained etched in its memory for as long as the murderers were not brought to justice. So, just as Blanche of Castile had urged, it was a matter of "cutting the head off the dragon", in other words, of destroying the citadel of Montségur.

The Crusader at Avignonet

The massacre of the Inquisitors at Avignonet

29

The fall of Montségur

In the spring of 1243, the royal armies encircled the mountain of Montségur. The siege looked like being a very long drawn out one. The place looked impregnable and the 400 or 500 people under siege within it seemed well out of reach of the crusading army. But treachery played its fatal hand in its demise, in the form of a guide who, one night, led a group of Basque soldiers up the terrifying, sheer face of the pog or mount. They set up a rock-throwing catapult a few score feet from the castle, which gave the assailants a huge advantage. The surrender of Montségur castle seemed a foregone conclusion from then on.

It was taken on 2 March 1244. The convicted heretics were burnt at the stake. The other believers were released, on condition that they confess the "error of their ways". The knights defending Montségur were free to go, and were not harassed over the murder at Avignonet. On 16 March 1244 the dancing blaze of the stake set for the *perfecti* of Montségur lit up the slopes of the mountain refuge.

In the Pyrenees, however, there was still a handful of undefeated fortresses, such as Quéribus and Puilaurens. The strategic and political importance of this line of strongholds explains the relentlessness and patience with which king Louis IX set about the task of conquering them.

Quéribus fell into the king's hands in 1255, followed before the year was out by Puilaurens castle, suffering the same fate.

Conclusion

The Albigensian Crusade started out as a religious war and ended up as a political conquest. The royal domain grew. The areas under the sway of the Trencavels of Béziers-Carcassonne and the count of Toulouse were forced to merge henceforth within the realm of the kings of France.

In 1249, Raymond VII died, leaving no male heir behind. His daughter, sole heiress of his possessions, was married to Alphonse of Poitiers, Louis IX's brother. The couple died in 1271, leaving no offspring. At that point, Languedoc became a permanent part of the French crown.

At the beginning of the 14th century, the Cathar heresy died out in Languedoc. Guillaume Bélibaste, the last known Cathar *perfectus*, was burnt alive in Villerouge-Termenès in 1321.

The castles in this Cathar country bear witness to those heroic, if bloody, times. They still stand there like so many symbols of a particular notion of perfection and freedom.

Villerouge-Termenès

Chronology

1165   The great debate at Lombers, near Albi, between Catholics and Cathars

1167   The Cathar synod of Saint-Félix-de-Caraman (now Saint-Félix-Lauragais); establishment of the four Cathar bishoprics (Albi, Agen, Carcassonne, Toulouse)

1208   Pierre de Castelnau, the Papal Legate, assassinated near Saint-Gilles

1209   **The Albigensian Crusade is launched by Pope Innocent III**
The sack of Béziers
The fall of Carcassonne; death of Viscount Trencavel
Simon de Montfort is appointed head of the Albigensian Crusade
First Cathars burnt at the stake at Castres (two *perfecti* burnt alive)

1210   Mutilation of the people of Bram
Fall of the strongholds of Minerve, Termes and Puivert
140 Cathars burnt at the stake in Minerve

1211   March: the fall of Cabaret
1 April and 3 May: siege of Lavaur; 300-400 Cathars burnt at the stake
May: Siege of Les Cassés, some 60 *perfecti* burnt alive
June: The first seige of Toulouse fails
August-October: the battle of Castelnaudary

1212   The Lower Quercy, Agennais and Comminges regions all taken

1213   The battle of Muret; death of Peter II of Aragon

1215   The IVth Lateran Council; Raymond VI, count of Toulouse loses his privileges to Simon de Montfort

1216   Death of Pope Innocent III, succeeded by Honorius III

1217   Raymond VI returns to Toulouse, to a rousing welcome
The second siege of Toulouse begins

1218   Death of Simon de Montfort before Toulouse

1222   Death of Raymond VI; Raymond VII becomes count of Toulouse

1223   Death of Philip Augustus, succeeded by Louis VIII

1226   Creation of a fifth Cathar bishopric, the diocese of the Razès
Louis VIII launches the Royal Crusade
Parts of southern France yield to the French monarch
Death of Louis VIII; regency of Blanche of Castile

1227   Death of Honorius III, succeeded by Pope Gregory IX

1229   Raymond VII, count of Toulouse, capitulates at Meaux. The Cathars go underground
The Council of Toulouse codifies the persecution of Cathar heretics at courts presided over by Dominican Inquisitors

1233   Pope Gregory IX entrusts the task of prosecuting Cathar heretics to courts presided over by Dominican inquisitors.

1240   The fall of Peyrepertuse

1242   Murder of two inquisitors at Avignonet

1243   Start of the siege of Montségur

1244   Montségur falls; numerous Cathars burnt at the stake

1249   Death of Raymond VII of Toulouse

1270   Death of Louis IX

1271   The countship of Toulouse is permanently annexed to the kingdom of France

1321   Guillaume Bélibaste, the last known *perfectus*, is burnt alive at Villerouge-Termenès

2

TOURIST ROUTES
AND SITES

CASTLES
VILLAGES
ABBEYS
CHURCHES
CAVES
LANDSCAPES

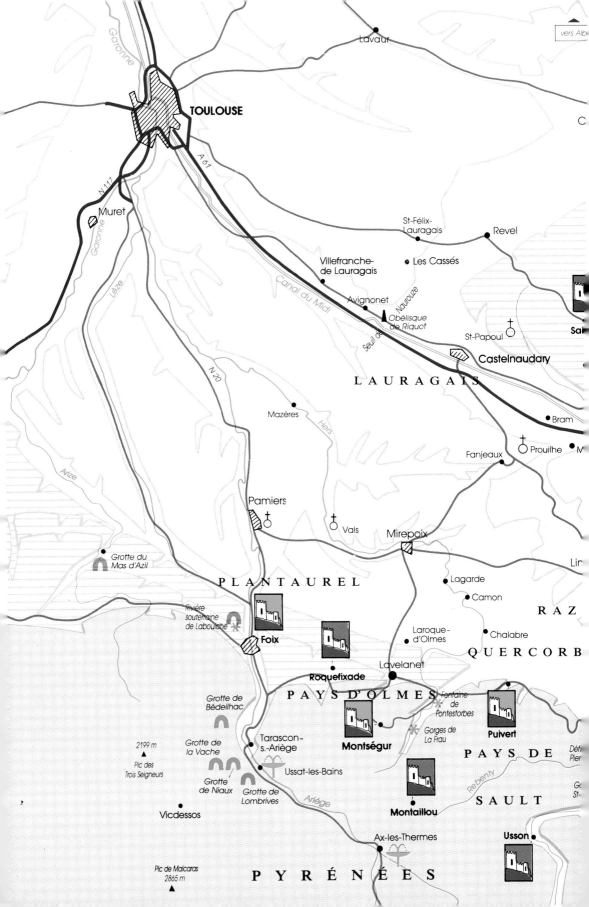

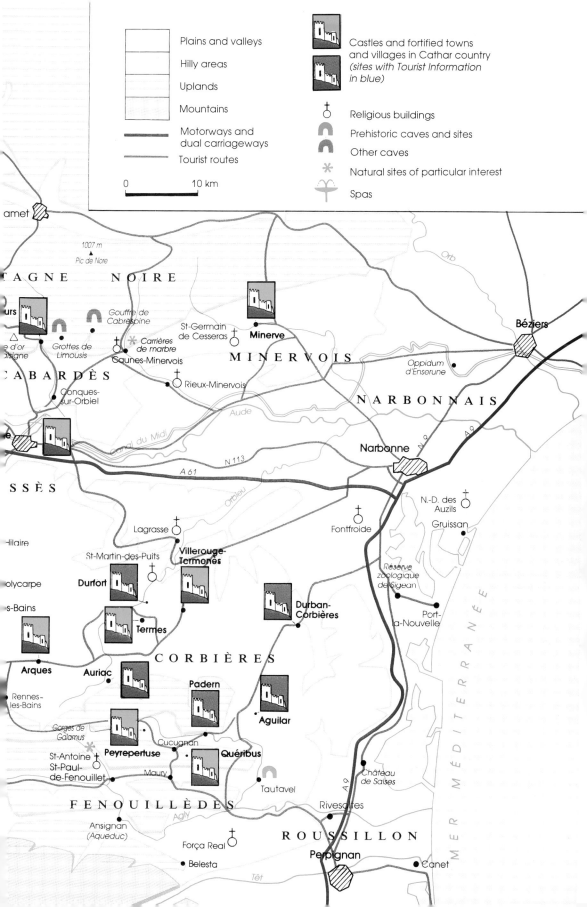

Legend

Symbol	Description
	Plains and valleys
	Hilly areas
	Uplands
	Mountains
	Motorways and dual carriageways
	Tourist routes

0   10 km

Castles and fortified towns and villages in Cathar country
(sites with Tourist Information in blue)

Religious buildings

Prehistoric caves and sites

Other caves

Natural sites of particular interest

Spas

---

amet

1007 m
▲ Pic de Nore

TAGNE   NOIRE

Gouffre de Cabrespine

urs

e d'or
lsigne

Grottes de Limousis

Carrières de rnarbre

St-Germain de Cesseras

Minerve

Béziers

MINERVOIS

Oppidum d'Enserune

Caunes-Minervois

ABARDÈS

Conques-sur-Orbiel

Rieux-Minervois

NARBONNAIS

Aude

Canal du Midi

Narbonne

N 113

A 61

SSÈS

Orbeu

N.-D. des Auzils

Hilaire

Lagrasse

Fontfroide

Gruissan

St-Martin-des-Puits

Villerouge-Termenès

olycarpe

Durfort

s-Bains

Termes

Réserve zoologique de Sigean

Durban-Corbières

Port-la-Nouvelle

Arques

Auriac

CORBIÈRES

MÉDITERRANÉE

Rennes-les-Bains

Padern

Aguilar

Gorges de Galamus

Peyrepertuse

Cucugnan

Quéribus

St-Antoine
St-Paul-de-Fenouillet

Maury

Tautavel

Château de Salses

FENOUILLÈDES

Rivesaltes

Ansignan
(Aqueduc)

Agly

Força Real

ROUSSILLON

MER

Belesta

Perpignan

Canet

Têt

Foix

From its perch at the top of a rugged crag, Foix castle looks proudly down over the town, which seems to be situated within a casket of rocks and greenery. The castle's elaborate curtain-walls are surmounted by three massive towers hemmed by machicolated battlements. Little is known about the original castle. In the early 13th century it figures on the seal of Roger Bernard, count of Foix, showing two square towers and crenellated ramparts. The round tower was added to the fortifications in the 15th century. The central tower of the count's castle contains three perfectly intact halls with ribbed vaults.

For a long time the castle was used for storing archives, and as a prison. Since those days, it has accommodated the Ariège Museum, which consists of two departments. The "Palaeontology—Prehistory and History" department boasts the skeleton of a large mammoth discovered in 1901 at Baulou, Ariège, as well as a variety of prehistoric objects, and exhibits from Antiquity and the Middle Ages. The "Arts and Crafts" department includes a faithfully reconstructed *ostal*[1].

The apparently impregnable stronghold acted as a fortress cum refuge during the Albigensian crusade. Although the count of Foix was not himself a Cathar, he offered fierce resistance to the crusading armies. He was quick to appreciate the perils threatening not only the heretic sect, which included many of his relatives and friends —his sister Esclarmonde and his wife Philippa were both Cathar *perfectae*—but also the entire region in general, and his own estates in particular.

Simon de Montfort mounted many an assault on Foix, but he never managed to take the castle. In 1215, however, the count of Foix eventually handed the castle over to the papal legate. The count repossessed the castle three years later, but when the royal crusade was over, he was forced once more to relinquish it.

In 1290, at the time of the merger between the viscounty of Béarn and the countship of Foix, the castle was abandoned in favour of the Béarn strongholds. It still retained a military rôle because of its strategic position on the border between France and Aragon.

During the 14th century, the most famous of the counts of Foix-Béarn, Gaston Fébus, was one of the most powerful noblemen in the South. When the Foix-Béarn family joined forces with Navarre, these southern barons became even more powerful. When Henry of Navarre became king of France, as Henry IV, the countship of Foix was fully incorporated within the French crown.

Gaston Fébus

Gaston III, count of Foix-Béarn, lived from 1331 to 1391, through the thick of what came to be known as the Hundred Years' War. Fébus was a name of his own choosing, after the sun-god Phoebus (Apollo). He was undoubtedly one of the great European princes of the West during this period.

He was a powerful politician, who tried to set up an autonomous princedom stretching from Orthez to Foix, across the foothills of the Pyrenees about which he sang so fondly.

He was also a courtly troubador, and as such left many famous works, both in *oc* and the (northern) *oïl*, and in Latin. For a very long time, his hunting book was a standard reference, as well as a model of remarkable clarity and detail.

Fébus was haughty, brilliant and cultured, but he also had an irascible and violent side. In all, he created his own legend as a fascinating courtly prince. His motto, which is also the motto of Foix, is well-suited to this image: *Tocas y si gausas* ("Touch me if you dare").

But Froissart, Fébus' contemporary, says it best of all in his Chronicles: "And I tell you that in my day I have seen many knights, Kings, princes and others, but I never saw any who had such handsome limbs, such a fine bearing, such a physique, his face beautiful, ruddy and cheerful, his eyes green and loving, wherever it pleased him to toss a glance."

1- The *ostal* was the sole living area in the ancient dwellings in the Vicdessos valley

The Caves of Ariège

Ten thousand years ago and more, human beings used caves situated near present-day Tarascon-sur-Ariège and in the **Vicdessos Valley**. These caves had been patiently hewn out by nature in the limestone strata of the Pyrenees.

Bédeilhac cave gapes like an immense porch (100 feet across, 50 feet high, and almost 2400 feet long). Its astounding dimensions turned it into an aircraft hangar in the Second World War. There are even those who swear they saw aircraft using it as a landing-strip! Huge stalagmites and stalactites vie for room in this enormous structure. In prehistoric times, the cave was inhabited. Various carvings, paintings and even clay bas-reliefs, like the bison with the foreshortened body, bear witness to this human occupation.

The **Niaux cave**s, created by now extinct subterranean streams, were occupied by prehistoric people as early as in the Magdalenian period, circa 14,000-9,500 B.C.

As you venture deeper and deeper into the bowels of the cave, the drawings become more frequent and strikingly more detailed. They culminate in the veritable works of art on the walls of the famous "Black Room" (Salon Noir), with its medley of bisons, horses, ibex and deer. Particularly outstanding are depictions of a bison with arrows, and a bison together with an ibex.

The **La Vache cave**, on the far side of the Vicdessos valley, is situated almost directly opposite Niaux. It is quite possible that these two neighbouring dwelling-places were occupied by the same folk, offering shelter for everyday living, and a place for spiritual, or even religious, practices. The La Vache cave has yielded a large number of remains, in particular carved bones, such as the example depicting a hind and fish.

In the limestone strata of **Plantaurel**, forming the pre-Pyrenean fold, water trickling downward has carved out a whole underground network of drainage and catchment.

The **Mas d'Azil cave**, north of Foix, is a gigantic natural tunnel excavated by the seeping waters of the river Arize. Even before man had had an inkling of the usefulness of this sort of site, large cave-dwelling bears, reaching over 8 feet in height, and mighty mammoths lived in such places. There is plenty of evidence of these creatures in the form of bear skeletons and mammoth teeth gathered in piles in one of the chambers. Homo sapiens claimed occupancy of this cave around 30,000 B.C. Its fame, however, is associated with considerably later remains, for it is the site of the duly named Azilian culture (10,000-7,000 B.C.). In a clear and interesting presentation consisting particularly of instruments and weapons such as scrapers, spears and even knives with flint blades, the Museum of Prehistory in the village nearby exhibits objects unearthed in the cave.

The **underground river of Labouiche**, a mile and a quarter long, has been made passable for visits covering a stretch of almost a mile. Boats are used, offering a fine view of the way water has eroded the limestone down the ages.

The **Sabarthès district** is renowned for its many caves, some still shrouded in the mystery perpetuated by legends that die hard. Is it not in one such cave that a handful of perfecti, escaping from Montségur in the nick of time, are said to have hidden the famous Cathar treasure?

Lombrives cave may not boast any rock paintings, but it makes up for this by offering a display of magnificent natural formations with picturesque names such as the Mammoth and the Petrified Waterfall. It plunges deep within the mountain, down to a subterranean lake, via a series of chambers and galleries.

This mysterious cave has attracted man from earliest times. Does not legend have it, after all, that it houses the tomb of the hapless Pyrene, who was enamoured of Hercules?

The actual shape of the cave is eye-catching. A soaring rock wall, 150-165 feet high, blocks the gallery and hampers access to the upper chambers, which can be glimpsed at the top. To get to them, ladders had to be fixed all the way up this sheer face. It is behind this barrier, acting at once as a shield and a frightening trap, that the famous mounds of human skeletons were discovered.

Was it Caesar who ordered the rebellious Gallic tribes to be so immured? Certain objects that have been unearthed among the human remains suggest as much. But it is not so straightforward to come up with a satisfactory interpretation of this ancient pile of bones.

One thing is certain, though: the cave itself witnessed many a dramatic happening, and deep within its dark recesses, it guards the fearsome atmosphere of places where the awful mystery of collective death still hangs.

Roquefixade

Five miles west of Lavelanet, the remains of Roquefixade castle mark the peak of an outcrop deeply hewn by erosion. A narrow path leads from the village below to the foot of the rocky crag, then climbs steeply around the northwest face of the cliff.

A huge natural cleft at the top has been filled in by the construction of an arch supported by the ramparts. The site was named after this *roca fisada*—fissured or cleft—as, later, was the castle, which was built in the 11th century, well before the crusade. The curtain walls, or what is left of them, hug the tortuous shape of the rock. Originally, they encircled an impressive keep built at the high point of the site.

The castle acted as a refuge for local people during the Albigensian Crusade, but never fell to the crusaders.

On a fine day the view stretches far off into the distance towards the eye-catching peaks of Saint-Barthélémy and the Trois Seigneurs, and includes the rock of Montségur. Is it not said that the wily denizens of this fortress communicated with those brave defenders of the castle of Montségur by lighting huge fires on the walls, which must have looked like so many lighthouses beaming out across the tossing sea of hills and woods?

Roquefixade became a royal stronghold at the end of the 13th century, to round off the line of fortifications built in the ranges of the Corbières, at the approaches to the countship of Foix, which was best kept under close watch. In 1632, Louis XIII travelled to Toulouse to attend the execution of the duke of Montmorency, who had risen up against Cardinal Richelieu.

He made the most of his sojourn in the region by ordering Roquefixade castle to be destroyed, for by now it served no purpose and was costly to keep up. Its ramshackle state illustrates the zeal with which the king's men tore the castle down in 1632.

Roquefixade castle

The Olmes district

The Olmes district is surveyed by the impressive mountain of Montségur. It is a land of contrasts nurtured by the twin influences of the Mediterranean and the mountains.

The village of **Laroque-d'Olmes**, 3 miles from Lavelanet, has a delightful 14th century church. The small chapel of St. Roch, at the high point of the village, was supposed to protect the inhabitants from the dreadful and frequent ravages of the plague, back in pre-Revolutionary days.

The **Frau gorge** is so wild that it bears the awesome name of "Gorge of Fear". Making your way downstream, you will come upon the **fountain of Fontestorbes** a mile or two from Bélesta. This "mad fount", so-called, is still a little steeped in mystery.

In the dry months, the flow from the spring slackens, becoming intermittent. When this occurs, the water level drops for half an hour or so, then rises again for fifteen minutes. This fascinating natural phenomenon gives the fountain a slightly magical quality, and you can imagine it peopled with elves, sprites and fairies.

The Olmes district

Laroque-d'Olmes

The spring at Fontestorbes

41

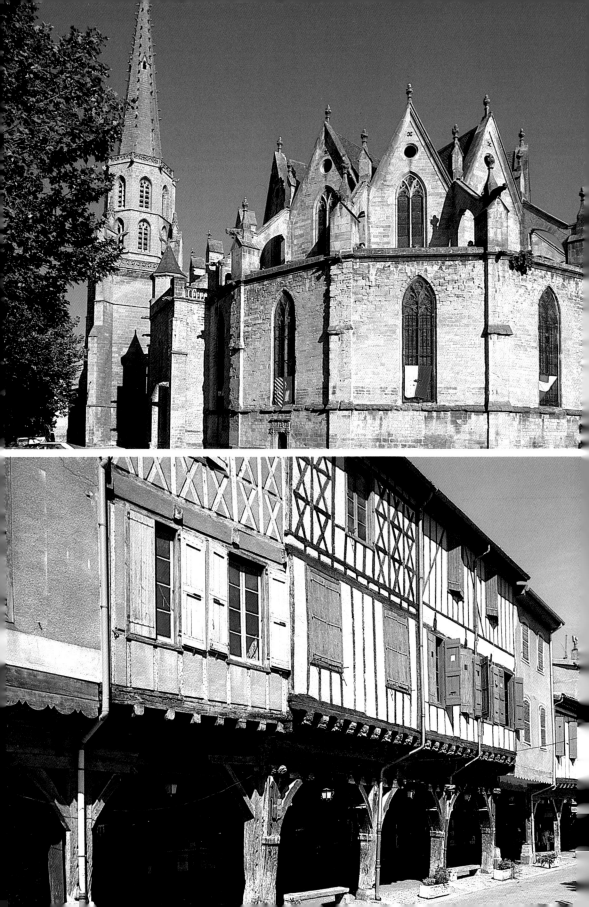

Mirepoix

This walled township nestling in the foot-hills of the Pyrenees boasts a mediaeval setting handed down virtually intact. It is a fortified town or bastide. The central square is edged about with covered wooden arcades supporting magnificent half-timbered residences.

The beams of the "House of the Consuls" are virtually original, with striking sculptures of human heads and monstrous creatures at each end. St. Maurice Cathedral is massive and imposing. It was consecrated in 1298, and underwent major restoration work in the 14th and 15th centuries. Its very broad Gothic nave (one of the broadest in Europe) posed enor-mous problems when the time came to com-plete the roof over it... in the 19th century! There is no transept, but a series of lateral cha-pels adjacent to the nave emphasize the buil-ding's grandiose aspect. The apse is covered by elegant pleat-like roofs.

During the 13th century, Mirepoix gave shelter to Cathar heretics, who founded several houses for perfecti in the town. Pierre Roger of Mirepoix, lord of the town, was an earnest Cathar. When the town was besieged, most of the heretics had already fled south to the nearby mountains. When the walled town fell, Guy de Lévis, a crusading knight and close battle companion of Simon de Montfort, recei-ved the order to set up camp in Mirepoix, the better to keep an eye on the thoroughfare bet-ween the Pyrenees and the Garonne lowlands.

In 1289, a flood destroyed the town of Mire-poix, then situated on the north bank of the ri-ver Hers. Legend links this disaster with the disappearance of the lake at Puivert, whose waters were apparently all of a sudden emp-tied. Under Jean de Lévis, the fortified town-ship was rebuilt in a safer site at the confluence of the Hers and the Countirou. But the town's troubles were by no means over, for it suffered sorely throughout the conflict erro-neously known as the Hundred Years' War.

The beams of the "House of the Consuls" in Mirepoix

Around Mirepoix

When the Albigensian Crusade was over, the Lévis-Mirepoix family were given **Lagarde castle**, perched above the small village of the same name. It was originally fortified to withstand assault, but creature comforts were added to it over time. Though partly destroyed during the French Revolution, its silhouette still stands starkly above the valley below.

The village of **Camon** lies snugly in the Hers valley, still the proud keeper of its legendary origins. Did not Charlemagne, no less, found an abbey on this spot in 778? The village subsequently enjoyed a period of prosperity, due in no mean measure to its monastery. The church and a few remains of fortifications are reminders of the age-old occupation of the site.

The town of **Pamiers** owes its origins both to its castle and to the 10th century foundation of an abbey dedicated to St. Antonin. Next to nothing of this latter remains today. In 1111, back from the crusades, Roger II, count of Foix, decided to build the castle of Apamea, in remembrance of the town in Asia Minor of the same name. All that now remains is the *castella*, a lush green hillock where the castle once stood. The cathedral of St. Antonin stands at the foot of the *castella*. It has been ably maintained since the 12th century, despite having suffered all the religious troubles down the centuries— Catharism, the wars of religion, Jansenism...

In the 13th century, the Cathar perfecta Esclarmonde of Foix stayed here. It was here, too, that Simon de Montfort drew up the famous «statutes of Pamiers», in support of the Catholic Church and its defenders, the crusading knights.

The village of **Vals** is an ancient Celtiberian oppidum or hill-town occupied since ancient times. The church, which is partly hewn out of the soft rock, has been skillfully designed on two levels. The inner crypt is richly decorated with Byzantine-inspired frescoes depicting the life of Christ (12th century). The upper level dates back to the Romanesque period, and the keep cum belfry is decorated with a fine discoid stone cross.

The mediaeval town of **Mazères** is a fortified bastide founded in 1252 on the rich estates of Boulbonne abbey. Like all such fortified towns, it has a distinctive, grid-like town-plan, with a system of straight streets intersecting with each other at right angles. The two buildings crucial to the life of any mediaeval walled town stand in the town centre—the church and the marketplace, this latter covered by a superb wooden openwork structure.

It is said that the famed Gaston III of Foix (Gaston Fébus) received king Charles VI in his castle at Mazères. In honour of the royal visit, he had the horns of a huge herd of cattle painted blue, echoing the armorial bearings of his own coat of arms: «Or, with two cows passing full face, horned and hoofed, conjoined and clariné in Béarn blue.»

Mazères is also the birthplace of the renowned Gaston of Foix (b.1489), duke of Nemours, who died in Ravenna in 1512. The castle and Boulbonne abbey were both razed to the ground during the wars of religion.

St. Antonin Cathedral in Pamiers

The wooden roofing over the covered market in Mazères

Montségur

Clinging to its so-called "pog" or pinnacle of rock, all of 3960 feet above sea level, Montségur castle guards its store of legends and secrets. As if driven wedge-like between rock and sky, its distant walls crown the towering dome-shaped peak of the huge fold formed by the pog. It would seem to be an impregnable stronghold, fortified by nature herself. The sheer rock walls, inhabited only by fragrant box bushes, leave nothing for it—if you wish to catch a glimpse of the citadel—but to strike out heavenward. And as you climb the steep slopes of Montségur, you may well be reminded of the commandments of a religion founded on purity and exacting moral standards.

The pog has been occupied since prehistoric times. Without the spread of Catharism in the lowlands and valleys over which it soars, it would probably have remained just another fortified site of little special interest.

The Cathars were well aware that their belief might be accused of heresy, and as such fiercely opposed. So they sought out a "Mont ségur" or "safe mountain", which would be both the spiritual hub of the Cathar Church and an unassailable fortress capable of sheltering persecuted brethren.

The lord of Montségur, Raymond de Péreille, turned the remains of rudimentary ancient fortifications into stout defenses. From 1232 onward, the site was justifiably known as a stronghold. It had a contingent of almost 500 people, some living in the castle itself, others in the small village built at the foot of the ramparts on dizzy-making terraces. The large number of archaeological remains unearthed on the site attest to much busy human activity.

Contrary to the claims made by certain authors, Montségur castle is in no way linked with any kind of sun cult. Any such beliefs were in fact quite alien to the Cathars. They rejected the material world as the work of Evil, and were thus barred from worshipping

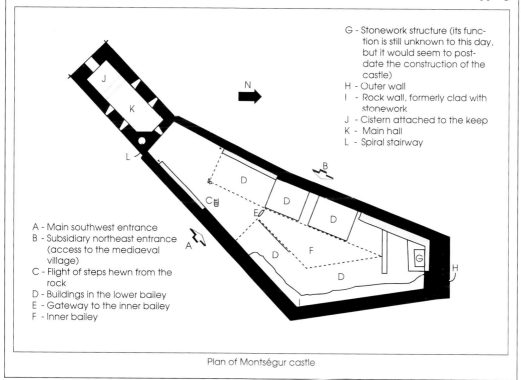

G - Stonework structure (its function is still unknown to this day, but it would seem to postdate the construction of the castle)
H - Outer wall
I - Rock wall, formerly clad with stonework
J - Cistern attached to the keep
K - Main hall
L - Spiral stairway

A - Main southwest entrance
B - Subsidiary northeast entrance (access to the mediaeval village)
C - Flight of steps hewn from the rock
D - Buildings in the lower bailey
E - Gateway to the inner bailey
F - Inner bailey

Plan of Montségur castle

the sun which illuminates the ills of this base world below!

What is more, the various archaeological excavations undertaken, as well as the studies of mediaevalists show more and more clearly that the castle now standing post-dates the Cathar period altogether.

If the design and construction of the castle were governed by a certain geometric dictate, this geometry was in effect the work of master-builders who traced the layout and elevation with measurements based on preordained formulae. These working methods bore no relation whatsoever to any esoteric intent.

The plan of the castle is simple, befitting a fortress, and makes the best possible use of the tortured shapes of the craggy peak. Every feature of military architecture from the feudal period is represented: a huge keep with its cistern, stout buttressed walls, forming an elongated central bailey, a single entrance gate, and a postern.

Montségur was indeed equipped to repel the assaults of the crusading army. But the Albigensian Crusade scored victories in the lowland regions, and Montségur remained a thorn of resistance in the side of king and Church alike. In 1241, Raymond VII, count of Toulouse, promised the king of France that he would destroy the rebel castle. But his siege was a flop. In 1242 it was Montségur that dispatched the small band of men charged with assassinating the inquisitors at Avignonet. The royal reaction must have been like a thunderclap. A new siege was laid in the spring of 1243. It would last ten months. On 1 March 1244, the crusading army managed to take up positions on the slopes of the pog, possibly even occupying the forward position on Roc de la Tour. Next day the castle fell to the besieging army.

After a fortnight's truce, the Cathars had to choose between renouncing their faith or being burnt alive. More than 200 *perfecti* and *perfectae* refused to recant. They all perished on a stake built at the foot of the mountain. A funerary stele erected in the Prat dels Cramats ("Field of the Burned") commemorates the sacrifice of the Cathar heretics.

Visitors who venture into the courtyard of Montségur castle feel protected by the tall walls. But, perhaps like those 13th century Cathar perfecti, they may also feel slightly detached from the world, confined within a hideaway of purity and perfection, entrenched in what has become the symbol of willing, and often even longed-for sacrifice. Montségur was eventually given by Louis IX to Guy de Lévis, and became a royal fortress. The castle was occupied until the 16th century, and then abandoned altogether.

The Archaeological Museum is the outcome of excavations carried out since 1958 on the site of the pog. The skeletons of two besieged occupants speak eloquently of the drama of Montségur. No less moving are the many objects displayed. These give visitors a better grasp of how day-to-day life might have been for those living in the castle and the village.

Montségur Museum: miniature head

The Prat dels Cramats or Field of the Burned

③

⑤

Puivert

Puivert castle, dating back to the 13th century, towers above its village on the road between Belesta and Quillan, still haughty up there with its square keep and fortified gate.

Like many a castle, Puivert was taken by the much-renowned Simon de Montfort and his army of crusading knights and soldiers in 1210, at the start of the Albigensian Crusade. But fire, blood and suffering seem things of the past now, and the encircling stones of the castle remind us more of the gentle and melodic minstrelsy of the troubadours. Merry-making and singing, to the accompaniment of the beguiling chords of viols and bagpipes, and long odes to love still inhabit the yellowing walls when summer breezes rustle the clambering ivy.

The large gaping windows in the keep offer glimpses of sweeping flights of stairs. The lords of Bruyères, who received the Puivert estates in fief, had their armorial bearings carved above the gates: "Lion rampant with tail forked and tied". The chapel incorporated neatly within the keep has magnificent vaulting with a fine interplay of intersecting ribs. The sculpted keystone is decorated with a virgin and St. Michael slaying the dragon. The six ribs are supported on cul-de-lampe corbels where strange figures brandish phylacteries[1]. Two handsome triple windows stand sharply against the deep blue sky.

In the "Minstrels' Hall", situated immediately above the chapel, eight ribs fan out from the keystone in the centre of the hall, finally coming to rest on eight sculpted cul-de-lampe corbels. The place is all the more bewitching when you discover that these sculptures have nothing whatsoever to do with war, or religion. Instead they depict eight musicians and their mediaeval instruments: the cornemuse, forbear of the Cévennes bagpipe called the *cabrette*, the vielle, later to become the violin, the tam-

---

1- Scrolls which used to bear painted inscriptions.

Armorial bearings

bourin, a narrow Provençal drum which has straddled so many centuries with such vigour, the lute, and the hand organ, not forgetting the psaltery, the rebeck and the cithara, all three now extinct. What refinement and sweet living those poets invented for themselves!

Legend tells of the daydreams of a certain Dame Blanche, in revery beside the lake at the foot of the castle. With inclement weather, the shores of the lake were inaccessible, and the princess requested that works be undertaken to lower the level of the water. And the outcome? The rocks that held in the water were apparently too weak, and collapsed... The waters of the lake burst through the breach and swept away everything in their path. Eight leagues away, Chalabre and Mirepoix were engulfed by the flood.

The Quercorb Museum at Puivert conjures up a comprehensive picture of both local history and bygone crafts, now a thing of the past. Designed to inform the visitor, it ably achieves its mission.

The Quercorb Museum

The Quercorb Museum in the village of Puivert will round off your visit to the castle. An explanatory model of this castle can be seen in the historical room.

The museum includes a fascinating room containing a display of musical instruments. Eight sculpted figures from the keep loom from the twilight, paired with replicas of their instruments. The Museum also recounts the history of the Quercorb district—the origins of its name, and the various decisive moments in its past, from the Middle Ages to the present day. The Quercorb of the 19th and early 20th centuries is depicted through the lives of its inhabitants. This was a pivotal period, when technological and economic developments altered craft activities and thus gave rise to a quite new society. Crafts that were once the proud symbol of their respective villages and villagers alike died out one by one--the wooden tub makers of Rivel, the chairmaker, the carders of the Hers valley, the wood-turners of Puivert, the cattle-bell makers, also from Rivel, as well as blacksmiths, craftsmen working jet and onyx... and many more.

A cithara player

Instrumentarium

Musician playing a portable organ

Montaillou

Since the historian Emmanuel Le Roy Ladurie published his book describing the mediaeval life and times of this small community, Montaillou has emerged from the obscurity of so many Pyrenean villages in the Ariège, to become no less than an "Occitan village" with 'celebrity' status.

It is situated on the slopes of Mount Aillon, at the top of which there is a large four-sided area, all that remains of Montaillou castle. But it was not destroyed by the ravages of the Albigensian Crusade, even if the heresy was present here throughout the 13th century.

During the 14th century, however, Montaillou did witness various sad occurrences. Between 1318 and 1325, bishop Jacques Fournier, the tireless inquisitor of the court of Pamiers, conducted a series of 25 harrowing cross-examinations. In these parts, all too swiftly suspected of religious deviation, theological and spiritual concerns were still very much in evidence on the agenda.

Montaillou castle

Usson

Buried deep within the labyrinthine Aude gorge, far removed from the fury of the Albigensian Crusade, the Cathar bastion of Usson castle now appears almost forgotten. It has been gradually crumbling ever since the French Revolution, and seems to have suffered the ravages of time more than the other great Cathar strongholds. Remnants of walls, gaping holes, and creeping vegetation give this site a dormant look. Yet, what tragic and thrilling events occurred in this hideaway! In 1244, the stake was already ablaze at Montségur when four Cathar *perfecti* slipped past the keen-eyed besiegers, and managed to vanish down the rocky slopes and make good their secret escape from the pog. Were they carrying with them that famous Cathar treasure, of which so much has been made? It matters little now. After an arduous flight through forests and narrow gorges, the fugitives finally reached Usson castle, hidden away in the uttermost recesses of the sheltering mountains.

Usson castle

The Aude gorge

In its upper reaches the river Aude is a Pyrenean stream, carving a hard-earned channel among the spurs and buttresses of the foothills.

St. George's gorge, plunging to depths of 1000-1150 feet, yet scarcely 65 feet across, has been hewn out by the river from thick limestone strata. The road could not be built until the rock had been blasted from one side of the river and the turbulent waters harnessed on the other.

The river then had to negotiate another rock barrier in its path. It managed to force a narrow passage which seems to engulf its crashing waters. This is the **Pierre-Lys defile**, where the sheer walls reveal no more than a sliver of sky above. It took much courage and time on the part of the flock of Felix Armand, parish priest of Saint-Martin-Lys, to drive a road through this ravine in the late 18th century. The road hugs the rock, clinging to the side of the defile with the limpid water way below. Where the river-bed is too narrow, three tunnels were bored. The last, called the "Curate's Hole", is a fitting reminder of the hard labour of those men who brandished pick and shovel, and finally completed their monumental task in 1887.

St. George's gorge

The Aude gorge

Puilaurens

Etched hard against the bright blue sky, well-preserved battlements and crenellations surmounting these castle walls form a geometric contour. Puilaurens is best seen in fine weather. It stands brilliant and resplendent at the top of a crag rich in luxuriant vegetation.

The castle's task was to keep watch on the upper reaches of the Fenouillèdes valley—an easy duty, because the only access road wound along at the foot of the breathtaking sheer overhangs on which the stronghold stands. Puilaurens is a perfect example of a military fortress, rebuilt and reinforced down the centuries, where, regardless of the chaotic present-day muddle, every structure, every recess and cranny had its rhyme and reason. How could such a castle possibly be taken by surprise? The huge soaring stone walls forced the assailant to manoeuvre within easy range of all manner of weaponry and war engine. If an enemy did manage to reach the fortified gate, how would he have avoided the danger posed by the slanting loopholes, raining razor-sharp arrows?

The outer yard or bailey is encircled by a wall surmounted by a parapet walk inside the battlements. This bailey protected a second even more fortified wall. The entrance gate was defended by a deadfall, a particularly graphic architectural term for a kind of chute built above gates down which stones and boiling water could be thrown from the top of the walls on to undesirable intruders.

The more accessible north walls would appear to have been reinforced by the addition of machicolations—apertures made in the top of the wall and used like deadfall chutes.

The square keep overlooks the rest of the castle. The well-preserved southwest Dame Blanche (White Lady) tower was fitted with arrow-slits and windows with sentry benches. From here an eye could be kept on the approaches and stepways.

The rarest and most unusual feature is the speaking tube running through the wall, which allowed people on two different levels inside the castle to communicate.

In 1243, after the death of the chatelain, Peter of Fenouillet, the castle was governed by Chabert of Barbaira, an ardent Cathar. He offered stout resistance to the onslaughts of the armies waging the Albigensian Crusade. While Montségur fell into the hands of the Catholic barons and watched the last flames flicker at its stake, Puilaurens still proudly withstood the crusaders. The castle did not in fact surrender until 1256, at which time it came under the feudal jurisdiction of the estates of the kings of France, along with Quéribus castle. If the truth be told, the aspect of the castle has changed a great deal since the Cathar period. As one of the fortresses defending the borders of the French realm against the powerful Spanish neighbour, Puilaurens had to be considerably rebuilt. Most of the fortifications date from this later period.

After the signing of the Treaty of the Pyrenees in 1659, which pushed the frontier with Spain back beyond the mountains, the castle was no longer strategically important. For a while Puilaurens was turned into a prison, before falling into gradual neglect. Then it became more and more of a ruin as people abandoned it to the fierce winds and the patient wear and tear worked by the passage of time.

The "five sons of Carcassonne"

From the latter half of the 13th century onward, the city of Carcassonne was, by royal command, the hub of a stalwart network of strongholds whose task was to support and protect the mother-city.

There were five castle strongholds in all, the so-called "five sons of Carcassonne": Aguilar, Termes, Quéribus, Puilaurens and Peyrepertuse. These five fortresses were formidable outposts protecting the southern reaches of the kingdom, close to the border with Aragon.

Peyrepertuse

This outstanding site is blessed by nature's own fortifications. Since earliest times, man has been well aware of the practical advantages of this soaring crag, which stands as a reminder of remote geological upheavals.

The crag rises steep and sheer to a height of 2625 feet. Mediaeval masons modelled and tamed the stone, fashioning it into enormous walls which merge with the bare rock of the pinnacle. As one, stone and rock thenceforth thrust skywards, showing off their finely hewn tooling against the blue above.

The castle appears inaccessible. A small, shady path, fragrant with the delicate scent of box wood beneath the fierce sun, leads as far as the barbican or gate-tower. Curtain-walls run the length of the sheer face. Vertical lines are the sole orientation as far as the contours of this place are concerned. What kind of mulish determination did it take to conceive of such a "fortress-within-a-fortress"?

On the eastern side, the outer wall is only accessible once you have passed through a small entrance gate guarded by a barbican. The way through leads into a narrow alley, impassable if entered square on. The bailey within this so-called lower wall is long and confined. It exudes a sense of shelter, protected as it is by well-preserved walls. The castle guards lived here. Hence the sink, latrines, and remains of buildings set against the ramparts, all reminding us that, then too, life was made up of little daily chores. They were physical chores, agreed, but still not to be overlooked, regardless of the majesty of the site.

The church of St. Mary was at once a place of worship—the impassioned theological debates raised by the inhabitants leave this in no doubt —and a place of refuge. As a keep cum chapel, it combines the simple elegance of Romanesque art with the fortification required of all such architectural structures. It is incorporated within a residential building called the "Old Keep", which provides access to the inner compound beyond.

The central enclosure here is much larger than the bailey inside the outer walls. This inner bailey in fact stretches right to the edge of the cliffs. Little is left here now, and the eye is immediately caught by another building standing on a narrow spur: San Jordi keep.

This is the classic "fortress-within-a-fortress", the last refuge. Haughty, silent and out of reach, it symbolizes the fierce pride of the knights of the Middle Ages. The steps leading to it—the famous St. Louis steps—seem to have been built wilfully right over a breath-taking sheer bluff. Who would risk attacking San Jordi across this flight of sixty odd steps carved from the rock, rough, as slippery as you could wish, and wheeling above the void beneath? You are still filled with a sense of danger here, especially when the wind tugs at you or howls in brief gusts, mocking your fear of heights. You earn your arrival in San Jordi keep. But once there, safe and sound, what an extraordinary view it offers!

Peyrepertuse did not experience any siege comparable to the massive onslaught launched against the citadel of Montségur. In fact, in November 1240, after lengthy negotiations, Lord William of Peyrepertuse acquiesced to the demands of the king of France. By surrendering, the fortress became another link in the defences arrayed along the Pyrenean border. When the castle had been completely taken, king Louis IX in person was swift to appreciate the defensive advantages of the place. He ordered the castle to be repaired and the citadel to be strengthened. San Jordi castle and the St. Louis steps date from this period.

A small force was garrisoned there until the French Revolution, but the Treaty of the Pyrenees, signed in 1659, marked the end of the heyday of Peyrepertuse.

All that the castle now withstands are the natural elements all about it—close by, the peaks of the Pyrenees, and far off to the east, the gentle shimmer of the Mediterranean Sea.

Towers guarding the entrance to Peyrepertuse castle ▲

▲ Peyrepertuse castle: an aerial view of the part called the "vessel"

Quéribus

As the eye strays east from Peyrepertuse across the topsy-turvy landscape of forest and vineyard, it alights automatically on the panoramic setting where Quéribus castle holds pride of place.

Against a sky so blue it might be purple, the citadel carved from the rock by some bold giant, or so you might think, seems to be set on a mounting of bare stone.

Uppermost, the castle is roughly cylindrical in shape. Below, a series of zigzagging walls, thick, stout and indestructible, winds down the steep rocky slope. The walls, in turn, are arduously accompanied by flights of steps suspended over the sheer drop.

Quéribus is truly a castle built in the air... with a view that seems to last forever, uninterrupted by crag or mountain. A watchman here could even see the gentle swell of the Mediterranean from this vantage-point.

Well before the epic history of the Cathars, Quéribus surveyed all the Fenouillèdes district, like some raised finger exacting obeisance. Then the region was set ablaze by the heresy and the bloody repercussions embodied by the Albigensian Crusade. Enclosed on high, and so remote, Quéribus still stood when Montségur was already no more than a legend.

It is worth climbing up to Quéribus in the midday sun, to see it balanced there on its rock foundations hewn out in broad steps... Three dovetailed, interlocking walls blend with and bolster the complex structure of the pinnacle. What an experience it is to venture into this last, narrow, tortuous bastion, with its machicolations, deadfalls and arrow-slits, and still guarding cool memories within its mighty walls. But the eye is drawn ever upward, to the keep itself and the sky above. What a massive place! Untouched by the wear and tear of time, many of its fortifications still stand. What kind of secret assemblies and discussions and schemes did these huge walls witness?

Quéribus castle on its crag

◀ Quéribus castle

The most handsome architectural feature of the keep is the Gothic "Pillar Room", so-called, where the impressive vault is supported by a single central pillar, which fans out in eight main ribs and four smaller intersecting ribs. Windows opening straight to the sky, chimneys, and stone benches all seem suspended in the dizzy void, reminding us that rock-falls and ruination can completely obscure the logic behind any construction.

Quéribus was the very last bastion of Cathar resistance to the crusading armies, finally surrendering in 1255. The fall of this last citadel, which openly espoused the concepts of Catharism, marked the defeat of Languedoc before the systematic campaign waged against the South by the northern barons. Thereafter, the Cathar religion was forced to go into hiding, stripped of all political and military backing. As the power of the monarchy waxed ever mightier and spread, underpinned by the patient and relentless proceedings of the courts of the Inquisition, so Catharism gradually died out.

The Pillar Room

Quéribus castle: an aerial view

Windows in the keep at Quéribus castle ▶

The Fenouillèdes district

The Fenouillèdes is a land of sharp contrasts between the Corbières and Roussillon. Its rich, green valleys, carpeted with vineyards, are surmounted by walls of rock—invincible cliffs and breath-taking crags.

The old **hermitage of Força Réal** (1) has undergone many changes, but its panoramic site still offers splendid views stretching from Mount Canigou to the sea.

The valleys here are colourful with the product of Fenouillèdes wine-growers. Sweet aperitif wines, blessed, as you might well presume, by these mild southerly climes, bear names extolling the sun on **Maury** and **Côtes du Roussillon** labels.

Both the land and landscape of the Fenouillèdes district are out of the ordinary, which might explain why it has been inhabited since the dawn of history. In 1971, the Caune de l'Arago cave near Tautavel yielded up a human head (2) that has since been dated at around 450,000 B.C.. Overnight, such a discovery turned this into one of the very oldest occupied sites in Europe.

Tautavel man... is no ape or primate, but is he really a man? He is standing upright, his forehead receding above heavy eyebrows, his jaw salient, all of which gives him a slightly determined look... And yet he is indisputably our ancestor. He has not yet learnt how to tame fire, that strange thing that now and then strikes the earth with an ear-splitting din. But as if to help us to a better grasp of who he was, he has bequeathed us scattered embryonic tools and weapons fashioned by his own hand (3). There was plenty to protect against: rhinoceroses, bears, and lions all ran wild in the Fenouillèdes!

Down the ages, settlement followed settlement. An ancient structure bestrides the river Agly —the **Ansignan aqueduct** (4), remains of an irrigation system installed by the Romans. It is a remarkable construction, at once sophisticated and practical— a fine example of the engineering skills of those canny invaders.

The limestone ranges, forming veritable rock walls, have dictated the orientation of the drainage system, with one notable exception. Over close on 2 1/2 miles, the Agly, as determined a torrent as it is powerful, has managed to hew out one of the region's loveliest ravines: **Galamus gorge** (5). The sheer, pale rock walls, a mere stone's throw apart, offer a tenuous foothold to the odd strawberry tree, broom and Kermes oak, clinging on high above the deep gorge below, where the water rushes through with much commotion.

The diminutive **hermitage of St. Anthony** (6) also clings to the rock face, hidden away among its clefts, offering just a glimpse of a tiny roof embedded in the stone. Winding dizzily above the void beneath, a flight of steps and an underground path lead to the hermitage. In this majestic natural setting, its solitude and isolation must have been well-suited to mystic and metaphysical contemplation of hermits seeking the absolute.

Sadly, the capital of the Fenouillèdes, **Saint-Paul-de-Fenouillet** (7), has preserved few traces of its past. At one time, from the mid-13th century to the mid-17th century, it marked the French frontier with Spain.

From Quéribus castle, towering 2300 feet above the plain, the eye hankers for a point of reference. To the north, but way below, the circular village of **Cucugnan** seems to trickle its jumble of orange-pink roofs down its curving hillock. Only the cypress trees, dark against the tremulous bright light, and the raucous cicadas seem to raise an energetic clamour against the distant sky.

When you stand on the crag of Quéribus and look down on the pretty little village of Cucugnan below, it is hard to resist singing the praises of the glowing, pale-coloured roofs. But the village, which is justly proud of its historic name, has a prouder claim to fame-- the stubborn legend of a priest immortalized by Achille Mir and Alphonse Daudet. And all the while, the sunned and vibrant vines wash in gentle waves against the crags roundabout...

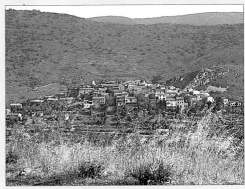

The village of Cucugnan

Aguilar, Padern and Durban

After the Albigensian Crusade, in the heart of the Corbières range, in what were once the "Spanish Marches", several castles were refitted by the king of France, standing like so many watchful sentinels keeping an eye on Aragon to the South.

From 1260 onward, in the wake of the bloody events which ravaged Languedoc during the 13th century, **Aguilar castle** fell into the hands of the kings of France, just when the Albigensian Crusade had finally achieved its goal—to procure the rich lands of Languedoc and include them within the royal domain.

The stronghold of Aguilar was incorporated within the formidable defensive system known as the "five sons of Carcassonne", whose main task was to keep a close watch on the kingdom's southern frontier bordering on the realm of Aragon.

Perched on top of a crag rising to 1300 feet, Aguilar castle surveys the various thoroughfares leading to the Corbières region.

Aguilar is an archetypal geometric castle. The 12th century central keep is surrounded by a hexagonal wall. This in turn is punctuated by semi-circular towers which were constructed during the 13th century.

The slopes of the hill on which the castle stands are not that steep, but are cleft by more rugged ravines to the west and south. This particular site gives Aguilar a certain harmony, which is enhanced by the vast expanse of vineyards which cloak the promontory.

Sturdy sprays of lavender give off their gentle scent within the ward itself, cluttered now with the rubble of stones that have fallen from the ramparts.

The small chapel dedicated to St. Anne rounds off the setting. It is a tiny Romanesque building of startling simplicity and unadorned austerity.

The ruins of **Padern castle**, once belonging to Lagrasse abbey, still dominate this region, which is now given over to intensive wine-growing. The castle was destroyed in the Middle Ages, but completely rebuilt in the 17th century.

The impressive ruins of the mediaeval castle at **Durban-Corbières** stand in a veritable sea of vines. All that now remains is a handsome façade decorated with elegant windows, which were added at a later date some time in the 16th century.

Around the mediaeval village at the foot of the castle there are still a few stretches of the 14th century town walls. A fortified gate, which is now a belfry, probably used to protect the way leading straight into the village and castle.

Wines of the Corbières

The wines of the Corbières—typically bold-hued red wines produced from famous grape varieties such as Carignan, Grenache, Terret noir, Cinsault and Clairette—are squarely in the good quality VDQS category: vins délimités de qualité supérieur.

The finest Corbières reds were granted their Fitou AOC—appellation d'origine contrôlée—guarantee of vintage in 1948.

These robust and fragant wines, perfumed by the Mediterranean, are produced in hilly vineyards in nine different villages—Tuchan, Paziols, Villeneuve-les-Corbières, Cascastel-les-Corbières, Fitou, Treilles, Caves, Leucate and Lapalme. To earn their AOC they must remain for at least nine months in the cellar.

Vineyards in the Corbières

1

2

3

4

5

6

The abbeys of the Corbières

The Corbières ranges form a rugged region issuing from the geological chaos ensuing from the slow but steady exposure of the Pyrenees. They have always attracted men and women keen to take their leave of the ordinary, overly busy, overly rowdy world below, and seek out havens of peace and solitude that lend themselves to prayer and meditation. During the Middle Ages, several abbeys built in the Corbières gradually earned a renown that spread well beyond the narrow confines of Languedoc.

Your eye need only come to rest upon the ornate 18th century portals of **Fontfroide abbey** to sense the importance of this architectural complex set and hidden so perfectly within a fold in the Fontfroide hills.

Aglow with the pink and ochre hues of Corbières sandstone, the abbey stands starkly against a solemn backdrop of cypress trees. The setting is truly magnificent, and the hush from the site as a whole inspires both respect and silence.

The Benedictine abbey was founded in 1093 on the estates of the counts of Narbonne. At the outset it was keenly governed by the strict rules of St. Benedict. Subsequently, it allied itself with the Cistercian order in 1143, and enjoyed a long period of prosperity.

In his efforts to check the advances being made by the Cathar heresy in the early 13th century, pope Innocent III chose two friars from Fontfroide as his papal legates. The murder of one of them—Peter of Castelnau—sparked off the Albigensian Crusade. Innocent III appointed Arnaud Amaury, another papal legate, commander of the crusading army... Either by some quirk of history, or to mark an abbey in full flourish, it was at Fontfroide that Arnaud Amaury finally gave up the ghost and was buried.

The abbey received many a donation from Olivier de Termes, originally opposed to the king during the royal crusade, but later a righthand man to St. Louis on the crusade to the Holy Land. He, too, asked to be buried at Fontfroide. Fontfroide abbey's long period of decline started in the 15th century, when it passed "into commendam" or lay hands. It was abandoned in 1791, but has been in private ownership since 1908.

Fontfroide embraces every feature of the archetypal abbey:

— Cloisters, lined by superb covered arcades with ribbed vaulting, supported by slender, finely sculpted marble columns.

— The elegant but simple abbey church with its Gothic vault and its shallow curving along each side aisles.

— The chapterhouse roofed by nine ribbed vaults, supported in turn on four fine marble columns.

— The monks' dormitory, situated right above the cellar.

This elegant, refined architectural complex is one of the jewels of this stirring region called the Corbières.

The Benedictine **Lagrasse abbey** has also known its moments of glory and great prosperity.

Legend has it that Charlemagne in person resolved to build an abbey in these parts, after a miracle had occurred. But the 8th century founding of Lagrasse abbey is more properly and accurately attributed to Nimphridius, a companion of St. Benedict of Aniane.

The abbey was built in the Orbieu valley on an outstanding site where, for centuries, the monks managed to install cunning irrigation systems.

The abbey is linked with the village by a 12th century humpbacked bridge, once fortified by three towers.

Until very recently, the abbey buildings and tower were occupied and maintained by a Catholic religious community espousing the Byzantine service. The whole complex is surveyed from all of its 130 feet by the 16th century tower which incorporates the belfry.

The small Romanesque church of **Saint-Martin-des-Puits** is of great interest, archaeological and historical alike.

The occupation of this spot is age-old, dating back to very remote times. Some of the columns would seem to be from Antiquity, and their capitals are of the Frankish Merovingian type. Pre-Romanesque remains of this order are very rare, which makes this little church a veritable architectural treasure.

A transept, consisting of two facing chapels, and a nave opening towards the choir through a superb horseshoe arch were added to the church in the Romanesque period.

A series of 12th century frescoes on the south and east walls of the choir, lastly, is another rare feature. The themes of these paintings are classical, and borrowed from the rich iconography of the Bible.

Villerouge-Termenès

A robust, four-sided castle, flanked by massive circular towers, rises above the gaggle of houses clustered close about it. The village of Villerouge-Termenès has kept its mediaeval soul intact, despite the passage of time.

The castle at Villerouge-Termenès once belonged to the archbishops of Narbonne, who undertook the task of renovating the building in the latter half of the 13th century.

In the early 14th century, when Catharism was dwindling in Languedoc, a handful of *perfecti* kept alive the memory of the heresy that had thrived so in the previous century. One of them, Guillaume Bélibaste, was arrested and burnt alive in 1321 in Villerouge-Termenès. He was the last Cathar *perfectus* to be tried by the Inquisition.

Termes and Durfort

A few stretches of wall and the odd corner tower perched on the rocky peninsula encircled by the river Orbieu remind us that **Durfort castle** once controlled the ravine that offered access up to **Termes castle**.

Colossal ruins are all that remain of Termes. What must this fortress have looked like, when its proud walls rose tall above the deep maze of the Termenet gorge, so awkward of access? The building was no less fearsome than the knights whose duty it was to defend the stronghold. In the 13th century, Raymond of Termes and his son Olivier offered shelter to Cathars fleeing the crusading armies.

In 1210 they put up plucky resistance to Simon de Montfort for the best part of four months, unbowed by assaults or the alarming engines of war arduously dragged all the way from Carcassonne. They were afraid of nothing and no one: Termes was reputed to be impregnable. But that summer had been tinder dry, and the autumn sun still shone fiercely on the fortress. So it was thirst that engineered Simon de Montfort's eventual victory: the emptied water-tanks forced Raymond of Termes to surrender. The relieved crusaders arrived to take possession of the castle, and were greeted by a shower of arrows... Termes was not quite ready to throw in the towel! A violent flash storm had replenished the tanks overnight. And the valiant defenders were able to hold out a little longer.

Then one evening a strange commotion gripped the castle. The men defending it were trying to slip away from the place, unnoticed. The alarm was raised, and the crusaders massacred the fugitives. These latter, weakened by dysentery, were no longer capable of repelling the assailants. So Raymond gave in, and the castle was finally taken.

After Simon de Montfort's death, Olivier of Termes managed to regain possession of his castle, but before very long he was once again forced to hand it over, this time to the king of France. Termes became a royal fortress, and was destroyed in the 17th century. A band of brigands had taken over the unassailable place from where they pillaged the entire region. Keen to be rid of these unwelcome guests, the king decided that the castle should be razed to the ground. The bill for the demolition work has survived to this day: it amounted to 14,922 livres (francs) and 10 sous. The detailed invoice was matched by the thoroughness of the job. Blown apart by gunpowder, the walls were reduced to vast piles of rubble.

All that now remains of this huge edifice are a few score yards of thick castle-wall. Originally, two concentric walls encircled the central keep, together with an adjoining building which is difficult to identify, but where—in some cruel irony of fate—a façade survives complete with an unusual cross-shaped window. This window, which seems to be stencilled against the blue sky beyond, recalls the bloody struggles in which those "fraternal foes", Catholics and Cathars, were engaged—for all that divided them was their interpretation of Christ's message.

Auriac

Auriac castle is now no more than a fragile lacework of stone silhouetted against the horizon, at the top of a steep crag that overlooks the river Orbieu.

Arques

The donjon or keep at Arques, in the rolling Rialsès valley, is unique among castles in Cathar country. There are no rocky pinnacles or sheer cliffs here, and this is no "breath-taking citadel". Instead, an atmosphere of gentle rural tranquillity prevails.

The tall 13th century keep stands solitary, hemmed in by its four perfectly intact corner towers. A spiral stairway leads up to all four of its floors.

This castle was built by the Voisins, a noble family who had settled in the region after the Albigensian Crusade.

Coustaussa

The sole remains of the fine mediaeval castle are a few stretches of pale stone wall, standing skeleton-like against the sky. Although the castle is more or less stripped bare, these eroded walls still exude an astonishing sense of power, and it is not hard to imagine them towering disdainful and mighty above the Salsa valley, keeping watch on comings and goings between the Corbières and the Aude valley.

Coustaussa castle was built during the 12th century by the Trencavel family. It was also a bastion of the Cathar heresy. Coustaussa was first besieged, then taken by Simon de Montfort's crusading armies, but for a long period it withstood the destructive instincts of men and the ravages of time. It was undoubtedly rebuilt at various times, before being finally demolished in the 19th century. In fact, it was lived in right up to the early years of the last century.

Coustaussa castle

The Razès district

This region has been well-known and long reputed for its health-restoring springs. In the out-of-the-way valley of **Rennes-les-Bains**, those famed builders and hot spring enthusiasts, the Romans, used the hot water, rich in sulphate, calcium, chlorine and radio-active properties.

Queen Blanche of Castile lent her name to the spa—"The Queen's Baths"—and was certainly not alone in her appreciation of the properties of its waters. Today, patients come in ever larger droves to regain their health in this resort.

The hot springs at **Alet-les-Bains** have likewise been developed and used since Roman times. Remains of pale ochre stone walls, as if raising arms to the skies above, mark the site of the ancient Carolingian abbey of Alet. It was destroyed during the fierce fighting that wrought such a bloodbath in the Razès district during the infamous wars of religion. The original complex must have been a model of might and harmony.

The village of **Rennes-le-Château** soars above the Aude and Sals valleys. Well-placed to keep watch on both the Pyrenean thoroughfare and the mountains above, this promontory was inhabited by man very early on. Because of its particular hsitory, this village, perched high above the surrounding lowlands, has been a source of both envy and awe. The 1960s saw the birth of the strange but persistent legend which tells of the existence of a fabulous treasure in this place. In the late 19th century, it would seem, a priest—abbot Saunière—unearthed this treasure as well as documents "so important that they might change the face of the world."

He shared his secret with his maid, Marie, but she refused to betray her master, even on her death-bed. Rumour has it that the building works undertaken at great expense by abbot Saunière had been financed by part of the treasure. The restoration of the church, the unusual Magdala library-tower with its goodly stock of books, the luxurious villa called Bethania, long journeys, banquets laid on in the priest's estates...True, all that must have cost a pretty packet! Certainly enough to stir the interest of the bishop of Carcassonne, who demanded to see the abbot's books. Unable to balance them, abbot Saunière was stripped of his priestly authority, and died not long after. From that day to this, Rennes-le-Château has seen some strange goings-on. Everyone seems to be keen to get their hands on the abbot's treasure. People "lend an ear" and auscultate, make soundings, and dig. Is it fact or fiction? mystery or hoodwink?

Whatever the case may be, the priest and treasure of Rennes-le-Château will enjoy their fame for many years to come.

Situated among its foothills, since Roman times **Limoux** has cleverly managed to make the most of its position of staging-post between the Languedoc lowlands and the Pyrenees.

For years this busy, hard-working town made use of the fast-flowing waters of the river Aude to drive a textile industry that now longer exists. Limoux still boasts the delightful atmosphere of a mediaeval township, encircled by its walls and dominated by the Gothic spire of St. Martin's church (6).

Its colourful carnival, to the strains of a unique musical refrain that is as short as it is obsessive, carries on an age-old tradition in a profusion of serpentine dances and confetti.

Another ancient tradition has to do with the production of that sparkling, bubbling white wine, dating back to the 16th century, which bears the name **Blanquette de Limoux**. The vineyards covering the sunny hillsides along the Aude valley have enjoyed a centuries-long reputation. Yields may be low, but what matters here is quality, not quantity. The fame of France's cellars is greatly enhanced by the inclusion of this warm and golden wine.

Saint-Polycarpe abbey stands in a small valley near Limoux. A monastery was founded here in 780 by a Spanish nobleman named Attala. It became a Benedictine abbey at the end of the 9th century.

The only part to have withstood the ravages of time is the fortified church, built in the latter half of the 11th century. It has a single nave, with no transept, leading to a choir lit by three semi-circular bay windows.

The vaulting is decorated with elaborate mid-12th century murals depicting scenes of the Apocalypse. The side chapels contain two 10th century Carolingian altars decorated with outstanding tracery. They also house the 14th century head reliquaries of St. Polycarpe and St. Benedict, as well as a monstrance, or silver reliquary, from the same period.

The nearby aqueduct, still standing, used to supply the abbey with water.

Fanjeaux

Perched on top of a rocky escarpment, the small township of Fanjeaux still retains its rank of spiritual and religious capital of the Lauragais region.

The village was chosen by Dominic Guzman, later to become St. Dominic, as the focal point for his preaching campaign waged against the Cathar heresy in the Lauragais.

The village still boasts various traces of that much troubled period:

— St. Dominic's house, where, tradition has it, the preacher was based and lived during his many stays in Fanjeaux.

— the Gothic-style parish church, built in the late 13th century, just as the Cathar heresy was dying out in the Lauragais.

— Prouilhe monastery, close by the village, founded by St. Dominic to combat the heresy not by force of arms, but by the persuasion of spiritual and theological argument. Nine Cathar women, converted by the man of God, took refuge there in 1206. The monastery was levelled during the French Revolution, but rebuilt in the 19th century, giving it its current architectural form.

As you leave the village and head towards Montréal, a Toulouse cross is carved on a stone forming the parapet of the bridge. It has been interpreted as a religious relic left behind by Cathar *perfecti*, but it now seems certain that physical representations of not only Bogomil themes but also of Greek crosses inscribed within a circle and of Occitan crosses with their circular motifs are all graphic representations wrongly attributed to Cathar communities.

Fanjeaux was the scene of considerable ideological and theological conflict, much of it bitter and fierce. Here, Cathar perfecti rubbed shoulders and vied with the most famous Catholic preachers of the day. So Fanjeaux remains the symbol of spiritual ardour and illumination in the Lauragais.

St. Dominic and the Dominican order

When St. Dominic (1170-1221) passed through Languedoc in the early 13th century—then a mere Spanish canon by the name of Dominico Guzman—he was struck by the advances being made by the Cathar religion in this region.

In due course he founded his first monastery in Prouilhe, near Fanjeaux, readily involving himself in several «disputations» with the Cathars. These were theological meetings at which Cathars and Catholics took sides against one another in fiery oratorical jousts. This was at a time when preaching and debate were still preferable to fire and sword.

The Montréal disputation, in the spring of 1207, was one of the most famous organized debates between Cathars and Catholics. St. Dominic, on the one side, and the Cathar perfecti on the other decided to defend their respective beliefs and refute the arguments of the opposite camp. Four referees would examine the statements and pronounce their verdict. Then it was that St. Dominic performed his most celebrated miracle. The Catholics had the idea of subjecting these antinomic texts to the ordeal by fire. The sheet of paper was cast three times into the flames, but it did not burn. Quite to the contrary it flew back out of the fire and was flattened, still flaming, against a beam in the ceiling, which it partly destroyed. The text written by the Cathar perfecti, on the other hand, was completely destroyed by the fire. As far as the Catholics were concerned, this was proof enough that the Cathar faith was indeed a heresy.

A half-destroyed beam was at some stage sealed into the wall of a chapel in the church at Fanjeaux. Legend has it that it is this beam that was touched in that spring of 1207 by the burning sheet of paper that had escaped intact from the ordeal by fire.

Faced with the ever-increasing vigour of the heresy, in 1215 St. Dominic decided to found a new religious order. The subsequent "Dominican order" was made up of friars whose principal other activity was preaching. Their role was to convince their audience, by way of explanation and demonstration, of the merits of Roman Catholicism, as compared with a doctrine which they were swift to define as the work of the devil.

Castelnaudary

This once small walled mediaeval village took the full brunt of the Albigensian Crusade. The battle of Castelnaudary in 1211 so marked the inhabitants of the day that the poet Guillaume de Tulède described it in his "Song of the Crusade" in the form of a grandiose epic in almost 300 verses. The battle was, indeed, a monstrous clash between Simon de Montfort's crusading knights and a coalition of Occitan barons who had finally joined forces against them. But the outcome of the battle was somehow inconclusive. The southern forces came within close range of Castelnaudary "covering the land like so many grasshoppers", in the words of Pierre des Vaux de Cernay. At the head of an undoubtedly valiant and determined army, though one that was considerably weaker in numbers, Simon de Montfort's position looked particularly shaky. Yet, by the time the battle was through, he had achieved the feat of completely routing the southern coalition. This by no means meant, however, that he had won the war once and for all. What had been shown was that it was, and would be, no easy matter to mount a consolidated joint force against the northern invaders.

Castelnaudary was already a small town built on high ground overlooking the Fresquel valley.

After lending its name to the famous battle, the small town grew fast, thanks to its bustling trading activities.

In the 16th century, Castelnaudary became the seat of an administrative division called a seneschalsy, and boasted a Presidial—a court that was at once civil and military. Parts of these premises were used as a prison from 1554 to 1926. The Presidial building has a fine Renaissance facade with decorative mullion windows. In the 17th century, when the Canal du Midi was built by the engineer Paul Riquet, Castelnaudary turned into a thriving and dynamic river port.

Castelnaudary

Saint-Papoul

The Benedictine abbey of St. Papoul was founded in the 8th to house the tomb of St. Papoul, the Lauragais apostle. It came under the aegis of the abbey at Alet until 1119. Later, in 1317, it became a bishopric, and remained as such until the French Revolution. The cathedral and cloister stand side by side, both dating from the 14th century. The cloister has superb colonnades with semi-circular arches.

The cloister at St. Papoul

Saissac

Saissac, northeast of Carcassonne, seems to have a faraway gaze, southwards to the Pyrenees stretching east and west. In the foothills of the Black Mountains (Montagne Noire), where the waters of the Vernassonne and Aiguebelle meet, the village and its castle stand on a steep crag hewn from the rock by these two streams.

All that remains of the castle are a few conspicuous post-mediaeval ruins, standing against the sky. In the 13th century, the castle was occupied by Jordain de Saissac. It was taken by Simon de Montfort's troops during the Albigensian Crusade. The village still has a good number of mediaeval houses with cantilevered façades. The old village wall has disappeared in places, but still includes its two cunningly crenellated square towers. The sweeping view from the village stretches to the Pyrenees.

Saissac castle

The Cabardès district

Villelongue abbey, south of Saissac, enjoyed renown and prosperity in the 13th century. Its cloister, once lined by beautiful colonnades with capitals embellished with flower garlands, animals and fabulous monsters, is partly ruined. The abbey buildings and, in particular, the majestic remains of the church offer ample evidence of the importance of this Cistercian institution in the Middle Ages.

The small village of **Conques-sur-Orbiel**, 10 miles from Carcassonne, has the remains of an ancient Romanesque fortified castle. Beneath the church's Gothic belfry, an unusual little passage still survives. The narrow, winding village streets have jealously guarded their mediaeval appearance.

In the 17th century, in the very heart of the small walled village, Colbert installed a textile mill. The building still bears the royal arms, struck complete with fleur-de-lis.

Conques-sur-Orbiel

The **Limousis caves**, lost in the garrigue scrubland, are situated in limestone terrain. The huge chambers house many splendid rock formations, including the famous aragonite 'chandelier', with its pure crystal whiteness.

The Limousis caves

The **giant chasm of Cabrespine**, situated in a region marked by very ancient limestone, not far north of Carcassonne, has been patiently hewn out over several million years by subterranean water.

The Clamoux river, running through the village of Cabrespine, flows into the chasm, carrying on its mammoth task of disintegration and construction in the depths of the huge cavern.

More than 10 miles of galleries and tunnels have been explored, but the chasm still guards secrets to be unearthed by speleologists.

Legend has it that some ducks were, quite literally, engulfed where the river goes underground, and re-emerged alive and well where it surfaces again at Pestril, near Lastours.

Now and again, legend and science will concur. Speleologists have in fact experimented by colouring the waters at the Clamoux collection station. These same waters then flow along a course in the depths of the underground gorge— which still remains to be explored in certain parts—before it then resurfaces at Pestril.

In 1988 an easy access point was added by means of a footbridge called the "Devil's Balcony". From the safety of this perch, visitors have a fine view of the amazing and ceaseless activity of the water in a landscape of karst.

Swirling erosion has carved out the "Giant Chasm Chamber" which houses a gigantic stalagmitic formation shimmering with different colours—white, ochre, yellow and red all jockeying for position. The bottom of the chasm plunges down into enormous rock folds which securely harbour the whole mystery of those dark abysses.

The "Red Chambers" are bedecked with a host of multicoloured pillars and red stalagmitic formations, after which these chambers are aptly named. The roof above bristles with aragonite crystals—clusters of graceful, seething concretions which project these dazzling white mineral needles in perfect stillness.

Last of all we come to the "Chamber of the Seventh Heaven", a mineral marvel in the form of a colossal geode resplendent with sparkling crystals, translucent stalagmites, elegant sprays of slender tube- and snakelike forms, eccentric shapes of aragonite, offering a chaotic frenzy of contortion which defies all the laws of gravity. It is a magnificent treasure trove where nature, in all her generosity, offers us a pure picture of her luxuriance and splendour.

Lastours

Like a team of tightrope-walkers balanced aloft on the pointed peaks of a long rocky ridge, the four castles of Lastours compete in daring with each other from their perch high above the Orbiel and Grésilhou valleys. A rock wall, 1300 feet long and just 165 wide, forms a site so outstanding that it has been occupied since those byegone eras dating back to prehistoric times. What foolhardy concept and what incredible arrogance were at work behind the decision to build four sister fortresses?

The most famous of them, **Cabaret**, is also the largest. The local lords were named after it, and it symbolizes the resistance mounted against the crusading armies, even if it ended up falling into the hands of Simon de Montfort in 1211.

The edifice itself is compact and functional. Elongated in shape, it consists of a many-sided keep, with adjoining rectangular residential premises. The rampart running round the edges of the high ground protects this central structure with its tall crenellated walls.

Régine Tower, the second castle, is close by Cabaret. It occupies only a small plot, and consists of a round tower flanked by a spiral stairway and a small wall, only the southern face of which still survives. Was this Régine or Royal Tower built after the Albigensian Crusade by the king's men? Its name would suggest as much, and all the more so because the earliest written references making mention of this building do not date further back than 1260.

The third castle, **Fleur-Espine** or 'Thornflower', occupies the highest point of the site, and is the most ramshackle. Does the mystery shrouding it reside in this spring-like name or in the tumbledown state of its walls?

The fact is that Fleur-Espine yields us little feel for a place that was once full of life. It stands on bare rock, and only the mysteries of its name now conjure up a passing flash of living memories.

Further down, as if breaking ranks, the last castle at Lastours, called **Quertinheux**, is situated not on the main rock wall, but on a solitary rock pinnacle close by. It consists principally of a round tower, like the Régine Tower, surrounded by massive and elaborate walls, as at Cabaret... Quertinheux, indeed, has all the features of a stalwart mediaeval fortified castle, but it, too, has suffered from the ravages of time, and its once impressive walls are in partial ruin.

The Lastours castles have certainly lost the splendour they once enjoyed. Yet the very name of Cabaret echoed for a long time like a challenge to the systematic conquests undertaken by Simon de Montfort during the Albigensian Crusade. The plan was doomed to fail from the start, involving as it did a simultaneous attack on three fortresses well protected by the sheer sides of the nearby valleys, and by a nobleman who may not have been altogether persuaded by Catharism, but who was nevertheless aware of the import of the campaign mounted against his direct suzerain, the viscount of Carcassonne. Simon de Montfort sensed the impending defeat, and decided against tackling the three castles of Lastours.

But he was keen to shake the impressive courage driving those defending Cabaret, so he staged a cruel ploy as part of the ruthless war that caused such a bloodbath in Languedoc. He had a group of prisoners brought to Lastours from the village of Bram. The men had had their eyes gouged out, and their ears, lips and noses cut off. They were led to Lastours by the sole prisoner who still had one good eye. But such atrocities failed to have the desired effect. The castles of Lastours put up further resistance and, paradoxically, it was not until the fall of the fortress at Termes, said to be impregnable, that the lord of Lastours in turn began to doubt his ability to withstand the forces fielded by the foe.

He surrendered in 1211, and the splendid fortresses of Lastours fell into the hands of Simon de Montfort, like so much ripe fruit.

Carcassonne

As a stronghold occupied since protohistoric times, Carcassonne conceals in its many-layered subsoil countless traces of busy human activity on its hill overlooking the river Aude.

It has in turn seen Gauls, Romans, Visigoths, Arabs and Franks, so, just like a history book, it holds within it the whole sequence of remains from those illustrious events that punctuate the region's past. Above all, though, Carcassonne remains Europe's most famous fortified city to have survived from the Middle Ages to the present day. It was undoubtedly the fated task of the walled city to preserve the various traces of this momentous period.

Legend has not scoffed at this outstanding site. The troubadors' epic songs and courtly lays tell us of the historic moment when the besieged city of Dame Carcass withstood the might of Charlemagne's armies.

Threatened by starvation, Dame Carcass had the novel idea of force-feeding the last sow with the last bushels of grain. The poor creature was then hurled from the ramparts, and burst wide open as it fell at the foot of the assailants. They were dumbfounded. Was the city then brimming so with food that it could squander its stores in such a way? If that was so, what was the point of pursuing a siege doomed to fail? And Charlemagne raised the siege. A triumphant Dame Carcass sounded the trumpets... whence Carcass-'sonne'!

In the feudal period the walled city became the seat of an almost independent principality confronting its Toulouse neighbours. The city suffered sorely from the violent attacks of the Albigensian Crusade organized against the estates of the counts of Toulouse who were keenly suspected of heresy. The viscount of Carcassonne, Raymond Roger Trencavel, followed a little later by his son, put up fierce resistance to the mighty barons from the North.

After 1240, the city fell into the hands of representatives of the French monarchy, who duly repaired it, the better to protect the kingdom's southern borders.

Twenty-six towers in all were rebuilt, as were the inner walls. This line of defence was then bolstered by an outer city-wall, punctuated by a further thirteen towers. All the defensive architectural devices known about at that time were used in Carcassonne: unassailable turrets and watch towers perched high atop the walls, posterns and barbicans or gate-towers for reinforcing the fortress's weak spots such as gateways, wooden walkways and machicolations designed for hurling projectiles at the attackers below, fearsomely effective arrow-slits and loopholes— in a word, a whole arsenal of technical features well-suited to the fighting methods of the day.

The count's castle itself, which was further protected by a deep moat and a barbican, became a citadel within a stronghold. The beautiful St. Nazaire cathedral was also rebuilt and enlarged. A transept and a Gothic apse, both lofty and tasteful in hue, were added to the simple, sober Romanesque nave, with its barrel-vaulting. At the same time the lower town founded by St. Louis without the city ramparts began to thrive, and burgeoned to accommodate its busy trading and business activities.

But in 1659, with the Treaty of the Pyrenees, the much-feared and impregnable walled city lost its task of keeping watch on the southern frontier. It was gradually abandoned to the ravages of time, and the destructive ways of men.

In the thick of the 19th century, dispatched by the Historic Monuments Commission, Prosper Mérimée and then Viollet-le-Duc were in turn dazzled by the majesty of the place, and managed to save the old city from complete ruin. It is possible to criticize Viollet-le-Duc for the excessive zeal with which he undertook the restoration work. Perhaps he left us with too ideal an image of a perfect fortress-city. But he must also be credited with bequeathing us the old city of Carcassonne—not a heap of rubble.

Carcassonne

The old city of Carcassonne, built on the east bank of the river Aude, is an oval fortified town, slightly elongated to the south.

The entrance gates:
— The Narbonnese gate (1) is the old city's main entrance. It is flanked by two massive, buttressed towers. A fortified chatelet and gatehouse or barbican round off the defences protecting one of the rare points of access to the city within.
— The Aude gate (2), also stoutly fortified by a barbican, chatelet and impressive machicolations, overlooks a stairway that is set between high walls.

The walls and ramparts:
The walls and ramparts consist of two concentric walls (3). The area between the two walls is called a bailey or ward (*lices*, in French). It is from here that you get the best idea of the scale and extent of the old walled city's defensive structure.

The parapet walk leading round the top of the ramparts is protected by battlements and crenellations, and includes covered wooden walkways (hourds) jutting out over the outer rampart walls, and designed for launching projectiles on the assailants beneath.

The two walls are punctuated by towers which give the whole *cité* a more cohesive aspect. There are 13 towers in the outer rampart and 26 in the inner.
— The northeastern Trésau tower (4) is a handsome edifice with vaulted chambers and Gothic-style windows.
— The tower of Justice is an elegant, rounded structure, and was reinforced during the reign of St. Louis. It had already served as a refuge for the Trencavel family when the city was under attack from Simon de Montfort's crusading armies.
— The tower of the Inquisition was, as its name suggests, the Inquisition's headquarters.
— The square Bishop's tower, straddling the ward, blocks all thoroughfare between the north and south ramparts.
— St. Nazaire tower is also square. Its postern could only be reached by a ladder that could be removed in the event of danger. Its task was to protect the basilica of St. Nazaire, situated right behind it. The present state of repair of this structure is the fruit of the restoration work completed in 1948.

The old city:
Inside the city walls the streets have retained the delightfully byegone look of a mediaeval town—narrow, winding lanes and alleys, half-timbered façades, and small squares transport visitors back to another era.

The count's castle (Château comtal):
The count's castle (6), a fortress within a fortress, dates back to the 12th and 13th centuries, but was built on much older remains, as is shown by traces of human settlements in the area adjacent to the Gallo-Roman wall (5). The count's castle was rebuilt during the Middle Ages and subsequently. It is a huge rectangular structure surrounded by a dry moat and protected by a semi-circular barbican or gate-tower. The castle proper consists of two large principal residential buildings and two courtyards.

The Lapidary Museum in the rooms of the count's castle contains an important collection of remains from the old city and the region roundabout.

The basilica of St. Nazaire:
This perfect example of religious architecture harmoniously blends the two major building styles of the Middle Ages. The basilica of St. Nazaire (7) incorporates both features specific to Romanesque art and typically Gothic details. The nave, which is the oldest part of the building, has a semi-circular vault of impressive simplicity—in pure Romanesque tradition. It stands in stark contrast to the light, lofty apse with its abundance of windows. Attached to the apse are six radial chapels lit by splendid stained-glass windows—outstanding examples of southern Gothic art.

The lower town (*ville basse*):
The town without the walls was founded by St. Louis after the Albigensian Crusade. It offers all the features typical of new towns constructed in the Middle Ages: a regular grid-like plan, dominated by the lofty tower of the church of St. Vincent; city walls, long gone now, and a moat that has been turned into wide boulevards; and a handsome central square.

Every year on 14 July the old walled city is «torched» with mock flares by skilled firework experts... The spectacle is fairylike and majestic—not to be missed (8)

Minerve

In the Causse or limestone plateau north of Lézignan, the Cesse and the Brian, both smallish rivers, carve a deep loop shaped like an elongated oval. In the broadest part, the promontory is occupied by the village of Minerve, which extends right to the edge of the cliffs overlooking the stony riverbeds beneath.

In the past, a fortress stood at the narrow neck of the promontory, guarding access to the village. All that now remains is the extremity of its late 13th century north counterfort, an ever-watchful sentinel towering over the crags. The village, fortified by nature and by the ring of walls which rise up above the sheer cliffs, huddles about its venerable church of Saint Etienne.

Minerve was a major Cathar centre. Its very site as a fortified village attracted a great many perfecti seeking refuge from the wrath of the crusading troops who had recently displayed such brutal ferocity during the sack of Béziers, in 1209. In 1210, Simon de Montfort's troops stood before Minerve. In this limestone terrain, beneath the dazzling sun of the South, the main concern of those besieged was their continued supply of drinking water. At Minerve, there was just one well. This was dug at the base of the sheer cliff towering over the river Brian. The sole access to it was afforded by a small fortified stairway from the village.

Simon de Montfort relentlessly pounded this part of the site, hoping to bar access to the well, and thus make his siege all the more devastatingly effective.

It took just seven weeks to bring this astonishing walled village to its feet! What could mere walls do against a patient campaign to undermine them, helped by a huge catapult positioned on the far side of the ravine? And what could the inhabitants do, wracked by thirst throughout the hot summer of 1210?

Viscount William of Minerve decided to surrender. His life was spared, as were the lives of his soldiers. But the heretics had to choose between renouncing their faith, or the stake! A hundred and forty *perfecti* and *perfectae* refused to deny their beliefs and threw themselves unaided into the flames of the stake built at Minerve, on 22 July 1210.

Those flames still seem to cast their sad glow when a setting July sun lingers on the roofs of the village houses.

The sculptor Jean-Luc Séverac has created an unusual piece of work to commemorate the tragic sacrifice at the stake in 1210. In a huge single block of stone he has carved the hollowed form of a dove taking wing. It is not a sculpture of stone, but rather one of air, and blue sky, assuming their own form and giving breath to this symbolic bird.

The Minervois Causse or plateau of soft limestone rock has been hewn and gashed and fashioned by the endless action of water. The result is an unusual variety of landscapes, including the two natural bridges carved out by the river Cesse near Minerve.

Minerve: a natural bridge

The Minervois district

In a sea of verdant vineyards, the small fortified village of **Rieux-Minervois** is famous for the extremely rare architectural form of its 12th century church.

This unusual building has a seven-sided central nave surrounded by a 14-sided rotunda-shaped ambulatory. Fourteen capitals, carved beyond doubt by the famous master-sculptor de Cabestany, are embellished with 12th century classical religious scenes.

The belfry that towers over the cupola is no less outstanding. It is a seven-sided tower with twinned bay windows.

Rieux-Minervois dates back to the Renaissance period and boasts the remains of a castle with huge towers. A fine 17th century three-arched stone bridge proudly spans the river Argent-Double.

The small town of **Caunes-Minervois** is renowned for its marble quarries north of the town, among the nearest spurs of the Black Mountains (Montagne Noire).

Marble from Caunes was used for the columns in the Grand Trianon castle, and for decorating the Petit Trianon at Versailles, as well as the Arc de Triomphe, the Carrousel, the Opera, and Chaillot Palace, all in Paris.

The abbey church at Caunes-Minervois, situated in the heart of the town, has a fine 11th century apse and two splendid towers, construted in the 12th century .

The elegant 11-12th century chapel of **Saint-Germain-de-Cesseras** stands at the foot of the Minervois Causse (limestone plateau), not far from the village of Cesseras.

Marble quarry at Caunes

The chapel of Saint-Germain-de-Cesseras

4 - Caunes-Minervois: the abbey church 5 - The church at Rieux-Minervois: capital ▶

Narbonne

The site upon which Narbonne stands has been occupied since earliest times, which lends the city a fame—and scniority that are unsurpassed.

Many remains bear witness to the settlement of this place in prehistoric times. As the capital of Roman Gallia Narbonensis, Narbo Martius was a thriving port from where the bulk of the produce from inland Gaul was shipped to Rome. In exchange, Narbo Martius imported the marble and ceramics that are so symbolic of the Roman civilization. The Visigoths, Saracens and the Carolingian Franks in turn established themselves here. Thanks to the activity of its port, the city remained prosperous until the 14th century. But the local rivers laden with alluvial deposits and sand gradually silted up the Mediterranean bay of old. The lagoons of Bages and Sigean remind us that the Mediterranean coastline has changed a lot down the centuries. Narbonne has lost its association with the sea. Since the 19th century its eyes have been turned inland towards its wine-producing back-country.

During the Albigensian Crusade, Narbonne was quick to learn its lesson from the tragic events suffered by neighbouring Béziers: it surrendered, and even struck up an alliance with the crusading armies, as early as 1209. The city soon became a crucial marshalling-point for crusaders arriving in the South via the Rhone valley. From Narbonne, they then fanned out throughout Languedoc.

Narbonne was thus at once the spiritual heartland of Catholicism in Languedoc and the military base for the crusading armies. As a result, it suffered relatively little from the campaigns undertaken by the crusaders.

The city has preserved an outstanding store of monuments from those mediaeval days.

The Archbishops' Palace forms a perfect part and parcel of the central complex, which also includes the cathedral of St. Just and its

Cathedral and Archbishops'Palace

cloister, and the Archbishops' gardens. As you enter this handsome architectural ensemble through Anchor Passage, the hushed but busy atmosphere of remote centuries calls to mind the power and splendor of the diocesan city.

The elegance of the Gothic cathedral, etched fair against the blue sky, is further heightened by the balance and harmony emanating from the cloister, sheltered by the impressive façades of the Old and New Palaces.

All the buildings seem to dovetail perfectly together, leaving nothing to chance in this maze of passages, stairways, inner courtyards, arcades and the gentle freshness of gardens.

This centre of matters religious, military, and political is nothing less than the extraordinary outcome of the patient and well-thought-out piecing together of a huge jigsaw puzzle, to which each particular century has contributed its own pieces.

Gruissan

Fanning out from the ancient fortified castle situated in the very heart of Gruissan— all that remains of it being the famous and oddly named Barberousse or Redbeard tower—the village houses, neatly arranged in concentric rings, form a mosaic of ochre and orange roofs right down to the water's edge.

Once a time-honoured fishing village, Gruissan has been long separated from the sea, and seems to have forgotten its maritime past, although the re-opening of the channel through the Grazel lagoon has stirred memories of brisk winds on high seas.

If you venture into the limestone wilds of La Clape heights, towering more than 650 feet over the shore, you will have a fine view of the lagoons around Gruissan, sheltering behind their coastal bars. On the trail leading through evergreen oak and cypress to the small chapel of Notre-Dame-des-Auzils, numerous steles faithfully guard the memory of mariners lost at sea.

Gruissan

Sigean

On the lagoon circuit, the small town of Sigean has lent its name to a zoo, opened back in 1974. It is more accurately called an African Reserve, because fully 80% of the fauna in it is of African origin. The major concern of those running the reserve is to offer each species as much space as possible, as well as a natural setting that is as close as possible to the animal's original habitat. Birds, reptiles, and mammals cohabit with large numbers of migratory birds who used this spot as a staging-post, well before the days of the reserve, on their flight south to the distant shores of southern Spain, and Africa.

A lion in the African Reserve at Sigean

Pink flamingoes in the African Reserve at Sigean

Béziers

Béziers stands proudly on its rocky promontory, surveying the river Orb below and, in the distance, the lush Hérault plain, carpeted with vineyards. Since time immemorial, the vine has been the wealth of Béziers. Pliny sipped these fine vintages in the 1st century A.D.

As a trading-post and crossroads, Béziers suffered a succession of attacks from invading Barbarians, Vandals, Visigoths, Saracens and Franks. They all coveted the handsome walled town, and established themselves in it turn by turn. The town was governed by a viscount and a bishop, to whom was added a city consul in 1131... just to complete the picture of a town divided between three opposing powers-that-be! The bloody sack of Béziers, during the Albigensian Crusade, has left a sorrowful memory of a vain and senseless act of barbarity. But the once walled town rose up again from its ruins to become a thriving city whose cultured middle class has made good money from a flourishing trade in wine, oil and wheat.

For all the troubles the place has known, from the wars of religion to the devastating wine crisis in 1907, its natural dynamism has always enabled it to emerge more vibrant and stronger than ever from the tribulations which it has bravely endured.

The lower walls of the cathedral of St. Nazaire are girded by rounded ramparts. The building retains the marks of alterations made to it down the centuries. It offers a clever admixture of Romanesque and Gothic art, enhanced by later additions in the 16th to 18th centuries.

A 14th century cloister stands alongside the cathedral, boasting beautiful colonnades with fine sculptures.

The old bishop's palace was rebuilt under Louis XIV, after a fire had seriously damaged the original building. Today, it houses the law courts.

The cool, shady Bishops' gardens are a perfect example of so-called «French-style» gardens, where nature is rendered almost motionless within the precise setting of a perfectly geometric overall design.

The *oppidum or* hill town of Ensérune

This fortified site has been occupied since earliest times, and beyond any doubt as far back as circa 600 B.C. There is evidence enough of Greek and Etruscan influences from the 5th century B.C., because much ceramic work imported from Attica and Campania has been unearthed there. In those days, the town occupied the summit of the hill with a checkerboard-like plan. It was protected by peripheral ramparts.

From 230 B.C. the town grew and spilled out beyond the ramparts as far as the old necropolis and towards the plain. At this point the influence of the Romans took over. There are countless archaeological remains of great interest. Some, like silos, cisterns, and house foundations are preserved in situ, while the Ensérune Museum itself exhibits objects discovered during different excavations undertaken since 1915. Judging from the itinerary drawn by Paul Riquet in the 17th century, the Canal du Midi would have run straight up against the lower slopes of the hill to the east of the Oppidum of Ensérune. Instead of having the waterway skirt round this obstacle, Riquet decided that the Canal should pass right through it. So he built a splendid canal tunnel, 567 feet long, right beneath the hill town, at the place called Malpas.

The *oppidum* or hill town of Ensérune

The Canal du Midi

Many people, from Antiquity onward, had dreamed of digging a water-course across the narrowest isthmus separating the Atlantic Ocean from the Mediterranean Sea.

In 1666, a minor tax inspector from Béziers, named Paul Riquet, embarked on precisely such a task... completing it in just 15 years!

Riquet presented his plan to Çolbert, Louis XIV's Comptroller-General of Finances, but he merely scoffed at what he called the southern tax inspector's 'obsession'.

Louis XIV, however, was always keen to bequeath to his realm works worthy of his splendour and greatness. So he entrusted Riquet with the job, even though all Versailles smirked at what was known as «Riquet's ditch»...

With that royal go-ahead, but pitiful technical back-up, work started on one of the 17th century's most ambitious construction sites.

Everything was a problem: raising the money, finding labour, coming up with solutions to the incredible technical problems facing Riquet. There was excavation and levelling work to be done; the canal had to fit the contours of the land; water had to be found to fill it, especially during the long dry summer months. Locks had to be planned and designed, as did series of lock 'steps' when the gradient was too long and steep.

Between Toulouse and the Mediterranean, the Canal du Midi has to cross the famous Nau rouze watershed. This is a low hilly area wedged between the Pyrenees to the south and the Massif Central to the north. It has forever been the unavoidable pass between the Mediterranean and the Atlantic. Riquet was well aware of this, and his canal took this same route. An obelisk was erected at Naurouze in 1827, commemorating this mammoth feat.

Through trials and tribulations, Riquet gave his all to his brainchild—his time, his own money, and his life. He died in 1680, just before the canal —his canal—was altogether finished.

The very next year, the canal was filled and the first lighters and barges plied between Toulouse and the port of Sète, 150 miles away on the shores of the Mediterranean.

The Canal du Midi is a veritable work of art, in both senses of the word 'work'.

Lined with 300-year-old trees, punctuated by its locks, crossing stout aqueducts, spanned by dozens of small stone bridges, the Canal du Midi forms, overall, a magnificent architectural ensemble. What does it matter, after all, if it can no longer be used by those huge barges of old! It recalls an era when passenger boats glided along at the speed of a horse walking.

The story of the Canal du Midi is well laid out in the Paul Riquet Centre in the small town of Avignonet-Lauragais—the very same spot where the two inquisitors of the Albigensian Crusade were murdered by Cathars from the stronghold of Montségur in 1242.

The locks at Fonseranes

The Canal du Midi

INDEX